# Therapy with Harming Fathers, Victimized Children and their Mothers after Parental Child Sexual Assault

Parental child sexual assault is one of the most hidden and complex forms of child abuse and one of the most difficult to guard against. This is the first book to provide an evidence-based approach to working with parental child sexual assault which includes intervention with the offending father, child victim, mothers, and other non-offending parents and family members.

Building on 25 years of experience with the Cedar Cottage Program, a treatment model aimed at working therapeutically with parental child sexual offenders and victims, this book is grounded in the authors' extensive knowledge as clinicians and researchers. Underpinned by current international research on the extent, nature and dynamics of intra-familial sexual offending and treatment outcomes, the model is fully described to enable understanding and implementation for new and experienced therapists, illustrated by extensive use of case examples drawn from clinical practice. By examining parental perpetrator tactics and behaviour in the lead up to child sexual assault, the chapters consider therapeutic approaches for child victims and families affected by parental sexual assault and aim to forge enduring safety for future potential victims.

Providing a comprehensive overview to working therapeutically, this book serves as an invaluable resource for supporting professionals in determining the best practice for long-term safety, whether the client is the child, offender or family.

**Dale Tolliday** OAM is the Clinical Advisor Sexual and Violent Behaviour, NSW Health and Clinical Advisor to the New Street Services within NSW Health. Dale's work with people who have sexually harmed others spans nearly 30 years. Dale's professional training is in Social Work and Law. He has a particular interest in training and professional standards for people working with those who have sexually harmed children. Dale is a member of the Australian Association of Social Workers and a founding member and past President of the Australia and New Zealand Association for the Treatment of Sexual Abuse (ANZATSA).

**Jo Spangaro** is a Senior Lecturer at the University of New South Wales where she teaches in the social work program. She is an internationally recognised researcher in the field of health responses to gender-based violence. Her research draws on over 20 years' practice and policy experience in domestic and sexual violence, with both victims and offenders. Jo is a member of the New South Wales Sexual, Domestic and Family Violence Council. Jo worked as a treatment coordinator at Cedar Cottage and later chaired the program's advisory board.

**Lesley Laing** is Honorary Associate Professor in Social Work in the Sydney School of Education and Social Work at the University of Sydney where her research and teaching focus on violence against women and children. Her research builds on policy and practice experience in community health, child and adolescent mental health, child protection and violence against women. She was founding Director of the Australian Domestic and Family Violence Clearinghouse and the NSW Health Education Centre against Violence.

# Therapy with Harming Fathers, Victimized Children and their Mothers after Parental Child Sexual Assault

Forging Enduring Safety

Dale Tolliday, Jo Spangaro and Lesley Laing

LONDON AND NEW YORK

First published 2018
by Routledge
2 Park Square, Milton Park, Abingdon, Oxon OX14 4RN

and by Routledge
711 Third Avenue, New York, NY 10017

*Routledge is an imprint of the Taylor & Francis Group, an informa business*

© 2018 Dale Tolliday, Jo Spangaro and Lesley Laing

The right of Dale Tolliday, Jo Spangaro and Lesley Laing to be identified as authors of this work has been asserted by them in accordance with sections 77 and 78 of the Copyright, Designs and Patents Act 1988.

All rights reserved. No part of this book may be reprinted or reproduced or utilised in any form or by any electronic, mechanical, or other means, now known or hereafter invented, including photocopying and recording, or in any information storage or retrieval system, without permission in writing from the publishers.

*Trademark notice*: Product or corporate names may be trademarks or registered trademarks, and are used only for identification and explanation without intent to infringe.

*British Library Cataloguing-in-Publication Data*
A catalogue record for this book is available from the British Library

*Library of Congress Cataloging-in-Publication Data*
Names: Tolliday, Dale, 1957- author. | Spangaro, Jo (Joanne) author. | Laing, Lesley, author.
Title: Therapy with harming parents, mothers and victimized children after parental child sexual assault : forging enduring safety / Dale Tolliday, Jo Spangaro and Lesley Laing.
Description: 1st Edition. | New York : Routledge, 2018. | Includes bibliographical references and index.
Identifiers: LCCN 2017054059 | ISBN 9781138286450 (hbk) | ISBN 9781138286467 (pbk) | ISBN 9781315268439 (ebk)
Subjects: LCSH: Child sexual abuse. | Abusive parents--Behavior modification. | Sexual disorders in children--Treatment.
Classification: LCC HV6570 .T65 2018 | DDC 362.76/86--dc23
LC record available at https://lccn.loc.gov/2017054059

ISBN: 978-1-138-28645-0 (hbk)
ISBN: 978-1-138-28646-7 (pbk)
ISBN: 978-1-315-26843-9 (ebk)

Typeset in Bembo
by Taylor & Francis Books

Printed and bound in Great Britain by
TJ International Ltd, Padstow, Cornwall

# Contents

| | | |
|---|---|---|
| *List of tables* | | vi |
| *Preface* | | vii |
| 1 | Introduction | 1 |
| 2 | The victim-centred family approach | 17 |
| 3 | Engaging the harming father | 32 |
| 4 | Mothers | 57 |
| 5 | Children who have experienced parental sexual assault | 72 |
| 6 | Siblings | 89 |
| 7 | Conjoint work within an integrated approach to therapy | 99 |
| 8 | Work with the extended family | 113 |
| 9 | Building safety | 122 |
| 10 | Group work | 139 |
| 11 | Creating safety for doing the work | 150 |
| | *Index* | 159 |

# Tables

| | | |
|---|---|---|
| 1.1 | Features of parental incest and implications for the child | 7 |
| 7.1 | Redirecting the mother's questions | 106 |

# Preface

The sexual abuse of a child by their parent is a profound violation of trust that has the potential for devastating, life-long impacts on the victimized child. It also fractures family relationships, in particular the mother–child relationship and the victimized child's relationship with siblings, but also relationships across the extended family. We wrote this book to share the knowledge gained over 25 years' practice by the therapeutic team at Cedar Cottage, the Pre-Trial Diversion of Offenders Program based in Sydney, Australia. This program was a unique collaboration between the justice and health sectors. It ensured that parents who had sexually abused a child were held legally accountable for their serious criminal behaviour while at the same time being encouraged to take responsibility by facing up to their victim and all others harmed about their abuse and the tactics that they had employed to establish the conditions for abuse, to conceal it and to avoid the consequences of discovery.

Establishing a program such as this takes considerable political courage to move beyond simple 'law and order' responses, which fail to recognize that few incest offenders are prosecuted through the traditional criminal justice system, leaving those victimized burdened with guilt, shame and divided family relationships, and potential future victims unprotected. The victim-centred, family approach to therapy described in this book aims to end the abuse of the victimized child; to protect potential future victims; and to repair the harms done to the victimized child and all family members.

Each author brings a unique history of engagement with the Cedar Cottage Program. Dale Tolliday was Director of the program from its first intake of participants in 1989 and subsequently to 2010. He was Clinical Advisor to the program until its closure in 2014 and remains Clinical Advisor on sexual and violent behaviour to NSW Health. Jo Spangaro was a Treatment Coordinator in the program for 12 months in 1994 and later Chair of its interagency advisory board in her role as Policy Manager, Child Protection and Violence Prevention for the NSW Health Department from 2000 to 2005. Lesley Laing, together with Bronywn Tuffy, wrote the initial proposal for the therapeutic program and later conducted doctoral research with fathers, mothers and children as they moved through each stage of the program.

We thank all team members who worked in the program and who contributed to the development of the practice wisdom captured in this book, in particular Beatriz Reid. We particularly acknowledge the women, children and men who engaged in the therapeutic program. We learnt much from your taking the risk of dealing with very painful experiences and betrayals. We hope that we have been successful in demonstrating that it is possible to work with all family members following parental child sexual abuse while keeping the safety – in its fullest sense – of victimized children and others harmed at the centre of all intervention.

# Chapter 1

# Introduction

## About this book

Parental sexual abuse of a child is a profound and devastating betrayal, which violates the child's trust, bodily integrity and sense of autonomy. It also disrupts and undermines the victim child's relationships with all family members. Without specialist intervention that both holds the harming father accountable and rebuilds the victim child's relationships with their mother and siblings, the risk of long-term emotional and social effects, including the victim's loss of family relationships, is significant. This book provides a victim-centred, family approach to therapy with families where a father has sexually abused a child. The approach outlined in the following chapters is based on the practice developed over 25 years at Cedar Cottage, a specialist, community-based treatment program in Sydney, Australia.

Although this approach works with all family members – the harming father, mother, victim/s, siblings and extended family – it takes a very different position from earlier family therapy approaches regarding the core issue of responsibility. Our approach holds the harming father totally responsible for the choice to sexually abuse the child and for the harm caused to the victim and other family members. It rejects notions that child victims or their mothers bear any responsibility for the abuse. It also challenges the view, dominant in the sex offender literature, that parental offenders are less dangerous than extra familial offenders because they are seen to present a lower risk of reoffending. Our perspective is that the parental role, which affords a sexual offender ongoing access to child victims and unique opportunities to enforce secrecy and evade responsibility, presents the greatest risk to children's safety, healthy development and well-being.

Following this introductory chapter, the book provides an overview of the principles and conceptual underpinnings of the victim-centred family approach in Chapter 2. The subsequent chapters describe the Cedar Cottage approach to work with each individual member of the family, before addressing the complexities – the 'how, when and why' – of conjoint work. This may involve sessions in which the harming father faces up to those he has harmed as well as

## 2 Introduction

sessions with family members who have become estranged through the tactics of the harming father: mothers and victimized children, and victimized children and siblings. Other chapters outline the ways in which future risks to children posed by the harming father can be managed following the end of treatment, including involving the harming father's extended family. For therapists who are not working with all family members, this book will assist them to keep in mind the ways in which each element of treatment needs to contribute to offender accountability and victim safety. Additional chapters explore the contribution of group work and identify the qualities that therapists need to bring to this field of practice.

We are committed to bringing the experiences of the families who participated in the Cedar Cottage Program into this book. We do this through the provision of case studies that reflect typical situations presented in therapy and through the anonymized voices of clients who participated in interviews with one of the authors in a study of their lived experience of attending the program in the aftermath of the discovery of incest (Laing, 1996).

## The Cedar Cottage Program

The Pre-Trial Diversion of Offenders Program, commonly known as Cedar Cottage after the location of the program, was established during the 1980s as part of a comprehensive New South Wales (NSW) government response to the growing recognition of the prevalence of child sexual assault. This included the establishment of a network of sexual assault counselling services for adults and children who experienced sexual violence, and legislative changes to address evidentiary issues for children giving evidence in court.

The establishment of the Cedar Cottage Program recognized the additional barriers that children face in disclosing abuse and participating as witnesses in prosecution when the abuser is their parent. It also responded to the limitations of the traditional judicial system in holding child sexual abuse offenders, and parental offenders in particular, accountable for their crimes (Cossins, 2010; Stroud, Martens, & Barker, 2000). Despite its title, the program was a post-conviction option. Importantly, diversion was not a form of decriminalization; it was an alternative form of prosecution in which the offender remained under the control of the criminal justice system, and traditional prosecution was resumed if he violated the diversion agreement (Cintio & Laing, 1987). If assessed as eligible for the program, the harming parent's guilty plea meant that his victim was spared participation in a criminal trial and cross-examination, where the attack on the child's veracity and motives increased the risk of secondary victimization (Cossins, 2010).

The program was a unique partnership between the health and justice sectors. Under the *Pre-Trial Diversion of Offenders (Child Sexual Assault) Act*, 1985, offenders eligible for assessment for entry to the program were: adults in a parental role with a child (under 18 years) whom they had sexually abused; and who had pleaded guilty to the sexual offending charge/s. Those who had overtly used force or violence or who had prior convictions were excluded. Entry also required the person to admit to the offences described in the child's police statement and to demonstrate some understanding about the impact of their behaviour on the child and other family members.

Offenders accepted into the program signed undertakings with the District Court and were bound by the terms of their Treatment Agreement with the program that outlined the conditions of participation. These included that they move out of the family home if this had not already occurred and have no contact with the victim or any other children without the express approval of the program. Breaching any condition of the agreement could result in their exclusion from the program and return to court for sentencing. A sample Treatment Agreement can be seen in Goodman-Delahunty (2009, pp. 178–181).

Despite the focus of the legislation on the offenders, it is crucial to recognize that the program was a child protection program, first and foremost, in which the primacy of protecting children was written into the enabling legislation. The purpose of Cedar Cottage's intervention with family members was to repair harms done, and provide opportunities for healing relationships fractured by the abuse, particularly those between the mother and harmed child and the harmed child and their siblings. The harming father was expected to facilitate this healing by actively owning responsibility for his behaviour and in this way relieving the burdens of guilt, blame and shame otherwise shouldered by the child and mother. In addition, the harming father was expected to make transparent the ways in which he had disrupted the relationships between other family members as a means to perpetrate abuse undetected.

Unlike many family therapy approaches to parental child sexual abuse, family reunification was not the aim of the program's intervention, nor were family members expected to contribute to the therapy of the harming father. In addition to facing up to the victim child, mother and siblings about the tactics by which he established the conditions for the abuse and manipulated relationships in order to conceal it, the harming father was expected to invite his extended family members into meetings at the program. The purpose of these meetings was for him to explicitly inform them about the nature of his offending and risk factors. In this way a wider audience, one which was likely to remain close to him through his lifetime, was fully appraised of his behaviour and of the ongoing risk he posed to children.

The program operated from 1989 to 2014 and had the capacity to work with up to 25 families per year, and in the time of operation received over 270 referrals. Of these, 131 were assessed as suitable following a six to eight week assessment period with the harming father. Of those accepted by the program, 83 men completed the program; 39 were breached for failing to comply with the conditions of participation (including to make satisfactory progress); and nine withdrew. An average of six family members per participant received counselling.

4 Introduction

In order to understand the approach articulated in this book we first explore the topic of child sexual abuse more broadly, and specifically the nature and effects of parental sexual abuse.

## Prevalence and gendered nature of child sexual abuse

The World Health Organization defines child sexual abuse as:

> The involvement of a child in sexual activity that he or she does not fully comprehend, is unable to give informed consent to, or for which the child is not developmentally prepared and cannot give consent, or that violate the laws or social taboos of society. Child sexual abuse is evidenced by this activity between a child and an adult or another child who by age or development is in a relationship of responsibility, trust or power, the activity being intended to gratify or satisfy the needs of the other person. This may include but is not limited to:
>
> - the inducement or coercion of a child to engage in any unlawful sexual activity;
> - the exploitative use of a child in prostitution or any unlawful sexual practices;
> - the exploitative use of a child in a pornographic performance and materials.
>
> (World Health Organization, 1999, p. 15)

Extensive prevalence research over the past 30 years has established that sexual abuse is experienced by many children around the world. Pereda et al. (2009) analysed 65 studies from 22 countries and concluded that eight per cent of men and 20 per cent of women have experienced some form of sexual abuse prior to the age of 18. Similar results were found in Stoltenborgh et al.'s (2011) meta-analysis of 217 prevalence studies published between 1982 and 2008, which identified prevalence of 18 per cent for girls and 7.6 per cent for boys. Consistent with these findings, an Australian study with a nationally representative sample of 1,745 young people aged 24 years, found that 17 per cent of girls and seven per cent of boys had been involved by an adult or older person in unwanted sexual incidents with/without contact before the age of 16 years (Moore et al., 2010).

### Prevalence yet invisibility of parental incest

Narrowing the focus to parental incest, large scale prevalence studies suggest that this is experienced by one per cent of children (Rosenman & Rodgers, 2004), though higher among women. Diana Russell's (1986) landmark study found that 4.5 per cent of her sample of 930 women had experienced sexual abuse by a biological/step/foster or adoptive father. A subsequent survey of 2,626 men and women, found that none of the men and six per cent of the women had been sexually assaulted by a father (3 per cent) or step-father (3 per cent) (Finkelhor, Hotaling, Lewis, & Smith, 1990).

Although indications from the USA suggest a decline in child sexual abuse since the 1990s (Finkelhor & Jones, 2012), the problem remains substantial. More recent prevalence studies report that 5.5 per cent of the girls and 0.6 per cent of the boys have experienced sexual abuse by a family member (Finkelhor, Shattuck, Turner, & Hamby, 2014). An Australian nationally representative survey estimated that, of the one million women who experienced sexual abuse before the age of 15 years, and where the abuser was a family member, 30 per cent were abused by a father (18 per cent biological fathers; 12 per cent step-fathers) (Mitchell, 2015). In this study, 42 per cent of the women assaulted by either their father or step-father were aged between 4 and 9 years when the first incident occurred. No breakdown by family member was reported for boys, of whom 28 per cent overall were assaulted by a family member, compared to 48 per cent of girls.

However, the power difference between parents and children, which the harming father can exploit to entrap the child and isolate them from other family members, makes parental sexual assault a largely hidden crime, as most victims do not disclose during childhood (Collings, Griffths, & Kumalo, 2005; Fontes & Plummer, 2010), and if they do, they risk being disbelieved and losing their family and face pressure to recant their allegations.

### Gender and child sexual abuse

Sexual abuse is perpetrated overwhelmingly by males. This finding is consistent across studies (Finkelhor, Hammer, & Sedlak, 2008; Stathopoulos, 2014; Stoltenborgh et al., 2011), with Finkelhor et al. (2008) reporting 95 per cent of perpetrators being male. Girls are more likely than boys to be assaulted by an adult (11.2 per cent vs 1.9 per cent) and for the assault to involve penetration (6.1 per cent vs 0.6 per cent) (Finkelhor et al., 2014). Other dimensions of child sexual abuse are also gendered. The mean age of onset of abuse was found to be nine years for both girls and boys, but abuse tends to continue longer for girls, ending at 14.8 years, compared to 13.4 years for boys (Briere & Elliott, 2003).

These gendered dimensions extend to familial child sexual abuse. As indicated by Finkelhor et al. (2014) and the Australian data reported above (Mitchell, 2015), and confirmed by other meta-analyses, girls are more likely to be sexually abused by family members than are boys (Quadara, Nagy, Higgins, & Siegel, 2015). Parental sexual abuse is also much more likely to be committed by fathers than mothers (Finkelhor et al., 2008). This was reflected in the experience of Cedar Cottage. No referrals and only one enquiry were received in relation to offending mothers through its 25 years of operation.

## The effects of child sexual abuse

Meta-analyses of the many studies of the effects of child sexual abuse document serious, long term negative consequences for approximately two thirds of children who experience it (Kendall-Tackett, Williams, & Finkelhor, 1993). These include increased risk for: substance abuse; obesity; depression; suicide; post-traumatic stress disorder; low self-esteem; and poor academic performance (Genuis & Violato, 2001; Kendall-Tackett et al., 1993; Moore et al., 2010; Paolucci, Genuis, & Violato, 2001).

The extent of negative consequences is influenced by a range of factors, including: the relationship between the child and the offender; the age and gender of the child and offender; and the frequency, duration and form of the abuse (Cashmore & Shackel, 2013). Older age at last abuse, a greater number of abuse incidents, a greater number of abuse perpetrators, penetrative assaults and how upset subjects reported being at the time of the abuse, are associated with higher trauma symptomatology (Briere & Elliott, 2003). O'Leary, Coohey and Easton (2010) found that being abused by a biological relative was one of three factors associated with more mental health symptoms in adulthood. Protective factors, which can mediate these effects, include family support and strong peer relationships (Cashmore & Shackel, 2013). When a parent commits the abuse, there is a reduced likelihood of family support, which makes long term negative consequences more likely. This underlines the importance of skilled intervention to prevent ongoing harm and the rejection of the victimized child by the family.

## Differences between parental and other forms of child sexual abuse

The most critical distinction between sexual assaults committed by a primary care-giver and other perpetrators is the way in which the developmentally dependant relationship between the child and both parents is undermined. Instead of nurturance and a secure base, a child who experiences parental incest lives with a fundamental lack of safety in their own home and bed, and is denied important sources of support that a child assaulted by a non-parent may be able to access. Parental assaults disrupt not only the relationship with the father but also other family members. Children who are harmed are typically separated emotionally from other family members by the deliberate tactics of the harming father, aimed at reducing opportunities to disclose and receive support as well as to discredit the child if they do disclose. Early work in this field by Elliott and Briere (1994) found that when perpetrators resided with the family, mothers were less likely to support the child, compared to when perpetrators lived elsewhere. We now understand that mothers are also subject to the harming father's tactics aimed at the deliberate introduction of distance in the mother–child relationship (Laing, 1996; Reid, 1998).

A harming father's tactics towards the child are commonly directed at undermining the child's confidence in the mother to act protectively. Statements such as 'She knows already', 'If you tell her she won't be able to cope/she will blame you/leave me' are typical strategies to deter a child from disclosing the abuse. At the same time harming fathers will often paint a picture of the harmed child that leads mothers to doubt their motives and truthfulness should they disclose. The reactions of other family members to a disclosure or discovery of abuse, particularly the mother is a complex area, further explored in Chapter 4.

A review of the research literature by Quadara and Nagy (2015) identified the factors that increase the harm experienced by child victims when the abuser is a parent. These include the gender differences outlined above, longer duration, greater frequency, earlier onset, more intrusive nature and likelihood of co-occurrence with other forms of abuse. As the review notes, these dimensions largely reflect the more extensive opportunities provided in the family setting, where there is typically wider scope for an abuser to develop coercive relationships and remain undetected. The review also found that intra-familial offenders progressed more quickly than extra-familial offenders to serious sexual acts (on average in less than 30 days). These dimensions speak to the heightened severity of assaults committed by parents and the importance of timely and skilled intervention to ameliorate the harm caused and to prevent life-long suffering. The common features of parental incest and their implications for the child who is directly harmed are summarized in Table 1.1.

*Table 1.1* Features of parental incest and implications for the child

| *Common feature* | *Implication for child* |
| --- | --- |
| Mostly in own home | No safe place |
| Secrecy | Full extent of abuse not known |
| Coercion | Child's submission compelled |
| More penetrative offences | Highly intrusive assaults |
| More frequent | Impact of repeated assaults over time |
| Longer duration | Entrapment of child |
| Critical relationship | Less/no support available |
| No safe parent | Insecure base – affects all domains |
| Family members less likely to validate (express belief of disclosure and empathize) | Child's experience is invalidated – processes impact alone |
| Concurrent safety issues within the family | General lack of physical and emotional safety within the home |
| Difficult for mothers and other family to challenge/process offender's denial | Disbelief and lack of support |

## Co-occurrence of parental sexual abuse and other forms of intra-familial violence

The harms caused by parental sexual abuse, outlined vividly in the preceding section, are compounded by the frequent co-occurrence of the sexual abuse with other forms of violence perpetrated by the harming father. In a study of 167 sexually abused children, Kellogg and Maynard (2003) found that 58 per cent of the sexual offenders against the children were physically abusive to their adult female partners and half were also physically violent to the child whom they had sexually abused. Based on an extensive review of available studies, Bancroft, Silverman and Ritchie (2012) estimate that roughly half of incest offenders are also using domestic violence against the child's mother. These abuses of power by sexually abusive fathers compound the emotional and developmental harm to the victimized child. They also provide a strong barrier against disclosure and can undermine the non-offending parent's capacities to respond if the abuse does come to light.

Some offenders will target a child who has a pre-existing poor relationship with her mother. When the child is experiencing emotional or physical abuse from her mother, this provides a further layer of protection for the harming father against the disclosure of the sexual abuse.

## Less dangerous than other sexual offenders against children?

The seriousness with which parental child sexual assault is regarded in the victim treatment field in terms of onset, intrusiveness, duration and co-occurrence with other forms of violence is in direct contrast with how parental sexual abuse is typically viewed in the field of sex offender treatment. For the past 20 years sex offender management has focused on re-offence risk using psychometric tools constructed from data drawn predominantly from incarcerated populations, the primary objective of which has been to identify high risk offenders (Goodman-Delahunty, 2014). Intra-familial offenders are typically determined to be low risk on static risk assessment instruments and are thus often excluded from sexual offender treatment programs. However, some research on the differences between intra- and extra-familial offenders has questioned the lower risk posed by intra-familial offenders, given the substantially longer period between the commencement of the offending and official detection (Eher & Ross, 2006).

We argue that there are four problems with the characterization of this group of offenders as 'low risk'. Firstly, ongoing and unfettered access to children means that a significant number of assaults can be perpetrated. Secondly, the considerable cross-over across adult and child, sexual and non-sexual offences means that the radius of impact of these offenders is wide. Thirdly, the particular barriers to disclosure and belief faced by children who are abused by a parent and the documented under-prosecution, mean that incarcerated offenders, on whom the risk tools are calculated, are not representative of this group of offenders. Finally, parental incest causes some of the most serious long term harm among all those affected by sexual assault.

## A note on terminology

We use the terms 'child sexual *abuse*' and 'child sexual *assault*' interchangeably throughout the book, seeing value in both descriptors. The word assault emphasizes the violent nature of this crime, while abuse is a broader term that captures the many harmful elements of this behaviour, beyond the physical behaviours, such as desensitizing a child to sexual material or touch, sexualizing a child's actions and imposing isolation or responsibility on a child.

As has been already established, sexual abuse of children is highly gendered, particularly in relation to perpetration. For this reason and for simplicity of reading, we refer to those who entered into the program for treatment as a result of their sexual abuse of children using the male pronoun. The terms *offenders* and *perpetrators* are problematic in the context of parental sexual assault. For the child victim, the person who harmed them is also their father or step-father, and often someone they love or at least remain connected to. As observed by Judith Herman (1981), it is the significance of the relationship between parent and child that renders sexual abuse such a betrayal. While we are clear that the actions constitute offences, we prefer the term *harming father*. *Offence* is an apt term for the behaviour, conveying the intent and criminality of the action. We do not use the terms *paedophilia* or *paedophile*, which we believe medicalize the behaviour, veering away from the adoption of responsibility, which is central to the Cedar Cottage approach.

Similarly, we refer to the victimized children as girls, reflecting the predominance of daughters in parental incest. At Cedar Cottage, all except three of the sexually abused children were girls, though we recognize that boys are also abused and suffer significant trauma from sexual abuse. We also prefer the term *victimized child* to victim, as the latter can be totalizing of the child, while the former acknowledges the actions of the harming father.

The term *non-offending parent* commonly refers to the mothers of children who have experienced abuse. Given the program's experience in relation to gender of the harming parents, we refer to these women as simply *mothers*, as they were all non-offending. Many of the children, however, had other non-offending parents with important roles to play, as discussed in Chapter 8.

We primarily use the term *parental child sexual abuse* to specify the form of incest being discussed in this book. When we do use the term incest, we are referring to parental/child abuse, rather than to abuse within other familial relationships.

## Contributing approaches

The Cedar Cottage Program drew on a range of sources in the development of its therapeutic approach. Here we briefly outline these early foundations, from which the unique approach described in this book was subsequently developed.

## The Child Sexual Abuse Treatment Program

The Child Sexual Abuse Treatment Program (CSATP), established by Henry and Anna Giaretto in California in 1971, was an internationally influential program that offered counselling to all family members following the disclosure of incest. The first thousand families seen by the program represented a cross-section of the local community, predominantly white, educated professionals. This challenged the widely held idea at the time that father–daughter incest was rare, and that it was primarily a problem of poor, minority groups with low intelligence (Giaretto, 1978). Giaretto (1981) proposed that the hidden and secret nature of child sexual abuse required the involvement of the criminal justice system in support of treatment, in part because abusers do not generally commit themselves for treatment and, further, that the families often seek to avoid the pain and distress that come with post-discovery interventions. This combination of criminal justice and therapeutic responses was an innovation that addressed the difficulties in prosecuting incest while also acknowledging the serious criminality involved.

Despite these important contributions, the Cedar Cottage Program did not adopt the CSATP's understanding of incest as a symptom of 'family dysfunction', in which the non-offending parents and child victims are seen to hold some responsibility for the abuse. We take the view that victims are never responsible for the abuse and that mothers are also victims of abuse and betrayal by the offender, and work with them proceeds on this basis, as described in Chapters 4 and 5. In reaching this perspective the victim-centred family model was strongly influenced by the work of feminist scholars and activists.

## Feminist scholars and activists

Second wave feminist theory understood relationships between individuals, families and the broader society to be oriented around gendered inequalities of power, privilege and status. Feminist scholars broadly, and those focussing on sexual violence specifically, centralized the concept of patriarchy, the system of social organization that maintains these gendered inequalities, as the cause of male abuse of women and children. Feminists argued that male dominance and ownership, and an ideology of women's inferiority promote the conditions which enable sexual and intimate partner violence to flourish (Bograd, 1984; Dobash & Dobash, 1979; Kelly, 1998). During the emergence of awareness about the hidden epidemic of sexual violence in the late 1970s and early 1980s, these voices countered the previously dominant individualized and psychiatric explanations for sexual and partner violence and initiated research that revealed the extent of violence against women and children.

### Judith Herman

Psychiatrist Judith Herman applied a feminist analysis to abuse of girls by their fathers, squarely placing responsibility for child sexual abuse with the abuser in

Introduction 11

her ground-breaking book, *Father–Daughter Incest* (1981). Herman countered the substantial literature claiming that sexual relationships between family members are not harmful, patiently documenting the serious effects of childhood sexual abuse. Nevertheless, she contended that permanent damage was not inevitable, mediated for some women by a supportive friend, family member or partner who assured them they were not at fault and helped them to integrate the experiences (Herman, 1981, p. 33). Another key contribution of Herman's was tackling the 'Lolita myth', that is, that father–daughter incest occurs in response to a seductive daughter. While accepting that children have sexual feelings, Herman made the case for the adult abuser being responsible for his actions, cataloging how the 'Seductive Daughter' is a fantasy used by abusers to justify their actions to themselves and others.

Herman also addressed the role of mothers, challenging the psychiatric literature which held them culpable for: being sexually unavailable to their partners; actively substituting their daughters as sexual partners; being 'unavailable to their children; and/or knowing about or tolerating the abuse' (Herman, 1981, p. 42). She coined the expression of 'entitlement' to sheet responsibility to the offenders, seeing this in terms of 'entitlement – to love, to service and to sex' (Herman, 1981, p. 49) and explored the ways in which father–daughter incest reflects a pattern of familial male domination and female caretaking, characterized as 'despotic paternal rule' (p. 63). This work was influential in shaping our understanding of the power dynamics inherent in offending, particularly in relation to children and mothers and led to emphasis on offenders working in their therapy to make these power tactics transparent to other family members.

Herman's subsequent work on complex trauma (1992) that identified the ways in which trauma resulting from betrayal and violence in family and intimate relationships differed from other types of traumatic experiences, maintained a feminist perspective, which differentiates it from some more recent approaches to trauma that have been critiqued for lacking a gender analysis (Tseris, 2013). Herman's emphasis on *disconnection* as an effect of trauma was especially relevant to the work of Cedar Cottage.

> [P]eople in the survivor's social world have the power to influence the outcome of the trauma. A supportive response from other people may mitigate the impact of the event, while a hostile or negative response may compound the damage and aggravate the traumatic syndrome.
>
> (Herman, 1992, p. 61)

This underlined the importance of engaging the non-offending parent, siblings and other family members in ways that rebuild the victimized child's familial relationships, which have been disrupted and undermined by the harming father.

## 12   Introduction

### Alan Jenkins – Working with men who abuse

In his work with men who have abused their partners or sexually abused their children, Alan Jenkins (1990) contended that our society is characterized by a gendered imbalance of power and responsibility where men predominantly hold power, but do not take responsibility for their actions, while women hold less power but shoulder responsibility for many social problems and tasks. This thinking informed the program's understanding of family dynamics in parental child sexual assault, particularly the typical power imbalance between the men who harm and their female partners.

Jenkins used acceptance of responsibility as a goal and organizing frame for work with men who use violence. Therapeutic engagement proceeded through a series of 'invitations' to the man to address his violence; to argue for non-violent relationships; to take responsibility for the abuse, his own feelings; and planning for relationships based on safety, respect and self-responsibility. Jenkins used the concept of 'readiness,' testing repeatedly whether offenders were 'up to' or 'able to handle' the direction of therapy, and in so doing, could harness alternative notions of masculinity. This invitational approach and the concept of 'readiness' were helpful for engaging men at the initial point of entry to the Cedar Cottage program, since it differed from the punitive and prescriptive responses that they typically anticipated.

### Narrative approaches to therapy

Based in post-modernism, narrative therapy is interested in the ways in which meaning is ascribed to experiences. The story or narrative is a metaphor for a way of organizing experiences through time (White & Epston, 1989). People seeking therapy are understood as engaged in dominant stories of their lives which are problem-saturated and in which they are out of touch with experiences of competence and strength. Through therapeutic conversations, unique outcomes, or previously neglected aspects of lived experience that contradict the dominant, problem-saturated story, are identified and explored and alternate stories are elicited (White, 2007). These ideas were usefully applied in the Cedar Cottage model, particularly in work with mothers and children, who were invited to notice and expand on stories of resistance and resilience. Similarly, response-based approaches to therapy also highlight the resistance of victims to oppression and abuse (Wade, 1997).

### Harm minimization literature

The Cedar Cottage Program also drew on the work on sex offender harm minimization, principally as proposed by William Marshall and colleagues, who understood the occurrence and maintenance of sexual offending as influenced by biological, behavioural, cognitive and gendered factors (Marshall, Laws &

Barbaree, 1990). The primary therapeutic focus involved changing cognitions that foster offending. Applying *harm minimization,* first developed for substance abuse treatment, the approach recognized that the risks of recidivism remain life-long and ongoing maintenance of risk management strategies is required by offenders and those around them. A strand of therapy, which the Cedar program employed with men who harm, is identification and modification of the *cognitive distortions,* which allowed them to establish, maintain and hide their abuse of the child/ren (Murphy, 1990). Earlier work drew on *relapse prevention planning,* which recognized that abuse is not impulse-driven behaviour but is carefully planned and executed over time (Pithers, 1990). Over the life of the program, contemporary developments in criminal rehabilitation were incorporated into the Cedar Cottage approach. Particularly influential was the Risk–Need–Responsivity (RNR) model (Andrews & Bonta, 2010, 2017), which identifies: risk level in order to decide the intensity of intervention required and the criminogenic needs that should be targeted. The responsivity aspect of the model has two elements: attention to the importance of the therapeutic relationship in the context of structured, cognitive behavioural intervention and the tailoring of therapy to the individual's strengths and characteristics (Andrews & Bonta, 2010). This fitted well with the holistic approach to therapy favoured in the Cedar Cottage approach. One area of difference is in the evaluation of risk. While parental child sexual assault offenders are regarded as low risk in comparison with other sexual offenders against children in the sex offender treatment literature, as described in this chapter the harm they cause to their victims and other family members is extensive and warrants the intense intervention outlined in this book.

The following chapter introduces the underlying principles and evidence of outcomes of the Cedar Cottage approach, in which safety remains the central organizing principle.

## References

Andrews, D. A., & Bonta, J. (2010). Rehabilitating criminal justice policy and practice. *Psychology Public Policy and Law, 16*(1), 39–55. doi:10.1037/a0018362

Andrews, D. A., & Bonta, J. (2017). *The Psychology of Criminal Conduct* (4th ed.). NY: Routledge.

Bancroft, L., Silverman, J. G., & Ritchie, D. (2012). *The Batterer as Parent: Addressing the impact of domestic violence on family dynamics* (2nd ed.). Thousand Oaks, CA: Sage.

Bograd, M. (1984). Family systems approaches to wife battering: A feminist critique. *American Journal of Orthopsychiatry, 54*(4), 558–568.

Briere, J., & Elliott, D. M. (2003). Prevalence and psychological sequelae of self-reported childhood physical and sexual abuse in a general population sample of men and women. *Child Abuse & Neglect, 27*(10), 1205–1222.

Cashmore, J., & Shackel, R. (2013). *The Long-term Effects of Child Sexual Abuse.* Retrieved from Melbourne, Australia: https://aifs.gov.au/cfca/publications/long-term-effects-child-sexual-abuse

## 14  Introduction

Cintio, B., & Laing, L. (1987). *Implementation of the Pretrial Diversion Program for Child Sexual Assault Offenders in New South Wales*. Sydney: NSW Health Department.

Collings, S. J., Griffths, S., & Kumalo, M. (2005). Patterns of disclosure in child sexual abuse. *South African Journal of Psychology*, 35(2), 270–285.

Cossins, A. (2010). Alternative models for prosecuting child sex offences in Australia. Retrieved from http://www.law.unsw.edu.au/sites/law.unsw.edu.au/files/docs/na tionalcsareformcommitteereport2010.pdf

Dobash, E., & Dobash, R. (1979). *Violence Against Wives: A Case Against the Patriarchy*. New York: Free Press.

Eher, R., & Ross, T. (2006). Reconsidering risk for reoffense in intrafamilial child molesters: new aspects on clinical and criminological issues. *Sex Offender Treatment*, 1(2), 1–9.

Finkelhor, D., Hammer, H., & Sedlak, A. (2008). Sexually assaulted children: National estimates and characteristics. Retrieved from https://www.ncjrs.gov/pdffiles1/ojjdp/214383.pdf

Finkelhor, D., Hotaling, G., Lewis, I. A., & Smith, C. (1990). Sexual abuse in a national survey of adult men and women: Prevalence, characteristics, and risk factors. *Child Abuse & Neglect*, 14(1), 19–28. doi:10.1016/0145-2134(90)90077-7

Finkelhor, D., & Jones, L. (2012). Have sexual abuse and physical abuse declined since the 1990s? Retrieved from http://www.unh.edu/ccrc/pdf/CV267_Have%20SA%20%20PA%20Decline_FACT%20SHEET_11-7-12.pdf

Finkelhor, D., Shattuck, M., Turner, H., & Hamby, S. (2014). The lifetime prevalence of child sexual abuse and sexual assault assessed in late adolescence. *Journal of Child and Adolescent Health*, 55, 329–333.

Fontes, L. A., & Plummer, C. (2010). Cultural issues in disclosures of child sexual abuse. *Journal of Child Sexual Abuse, 19*(5), 491–518. doi:10.1080/10538712.2010.512520

Genuis, M. L., & Violato, C. (2001). A meta-analysis of the published research on the effects of child sexual abuse. *The Journal of Psychology*, 135(1), 17–17–36.

Giaretto, H. (1978). Humanistic treatment of father-daughter incest. *Journal of Humanistic Psychology*, 18(4), 59–76.

Giaretto, H. (1981). A comprehensive child sexual treatment program. In P. Beezley-Mrazek & H. Kempe (Eds.), *Sexually Abused Children and their Families*. Oxford: Pergamon Press.

Goodman-Delahunty, J. (2009). The NSW Pre-Trial Diversion of Offenders (Child Sexual Assault) Program: An evaluation of treatment outcomes. Retrieved from https://www.researchgate.net/publication/298788143_The_NSW_Pre-trial_Diversion_of_Offen ders_Child_Sexual_Assault_Program_An_evaluation_of_treatment_outcomes

Goodman-Delahunty, J. (2014). Profiling parental child sex abuse. *Trends & Issues in Crime and Criminal Justice*. Retrieved from http://www.aic.gov.au/media_library/publications/tandi_pdf/tandi465.pdf

Herman, J. L. (1981). *Father–Daughter Incest*. Cambridge, Mass: Harvard University Press.

Herman, J. L. (1992). *Trauma and Recovery*. USA: Basic Books.

Jenkins, A. (1990). *Invitations to Responsibility: The Therapeutic Engagement of Men who are Violent and Abusive*. Adelaide: South Australia Dulwich Centre Publications.

Kelly, L. (1998). *Surviving Sexual Violence*. Oxford: Oxford Polity Press.

Kellogg, N. D., & Menard, S. W. (2003). Violence among family members of children and adolescents evaluated for sexual abuse. *Child Abuse & Neglect*, 27(12), 1367–1376. doi:10.1016/j.chiabu.2003.10.008

Kendall-Tackett, K., Williams, L. M., & Finkelhor, D. (1993). Impact of sexual abuse on children: A review and synthesis of recent empirical studies. *Psychological Bulletin,* 113(1), 164–180. doi:10.1037/0033-2909.113.1.164

Laing, L. (1996). *Unravelling Responsibility: Incest Offenders, Mothers, and Victims in Treatment.* (PhD), The University of New South Wales, Sydney.

Marshall, W., Laws, D. R., & Barbaree, H. (1990). *Handbook of Sexual Assault: Issues, Theories, and Treatment of the Offender.* New York: Plenum Press.

Mitchell, M. (2015, 14 October). *Children's Rights Report.* Retrieved from https://www. humanrights.gov.au/our-work/childrens-rights/publications/childrens-rights-report-2015

Moore, E., Romaniuka, H., Olsson, C., Jayasinghea, Y., Carlina, J., & Patton, G. (2010). The prevalence of childhood sexual abuse and adolescent unwanted sexual contact among boys and girls living in Victoria, Australia. *Child Abuse & Neglect,* 34(5), 379–385.

Murphy, W. (1990). Assessment and modification of cognitive distortions with sex offenders. In W. Marshall, D. R. Laws, & H. Barbaree (Eds.), *Handbook of Sexual Assault: Issues, Theories, and Treatment of the Offender* (pp. 331–342). New York: Plenum Press.

O'Leary, P., Coohey, C., & Easton, S. (2010). The effect of severe child sexual abuse and disclosure on mental health during adulthood. *Journal of Child Sexual Abuse,* 19(3), 275–289.

Paolucci, E. O., Genuis, M. L., & ViolatoC. (2001). A meta-analysis of the published research on the effects of child sexual abuse. *Journal of Psychology,* 135(1), 17–36.

Pereda, N., Georgina Guiler, Maria Forns, & Gómez-Benito, J. (2009). The prevalence of child sexual abuse in community and student samples: A meta-analysis. *Clinical Psychology Review,* 29(4), 328–338.

Pithers, W. (1990). Relapse prevention with sexual aggressors: A method for maintaining therapeutic gain and enhancing external supervision. In W. Marshall, D. R. Laws, & H. E. Barbaree (Eds.), *A Handbook of Sexual Assault: Issues, Theories, and Treatment of the Offender* (pp. 343–362). New York: Plenum Press.

Quadara, A., Nagy, V., Higgins, D., & Siegel, N. (2015). *Conceptualising the Prevention of Child Sexual Abuse – Final Report. Research Report.* Retrieved from https://aifs.gov. au/publications/conceptualising-prevention-child-sexual-abuse

Reid, B. (1998). *An Exploration of Tactics used by Perpetrators of Intrafamilial Child Sexual Assault.* (PhD), University of New South Wales Sydney, Australia. Retrieved from http://www.unsworks.unsw.edu.au/primo_library/libweb/action/dlDisplay.do?vid= UNSWORKS&docId=unsworks_40041

Rosenman, S., & Rodgers, B. (2004). Childhood adversity in an Australian population. *Social Psychiatry and Psychiatric Epidemiology,* 39(9), 695–702.

Russell, D. (1986). *The Secret Trauma: Incest in the Lives of Girls and Women.* New York: Basic Books.

Stathopoulos, M. (2014, March). The exception that proves the rule: Female sex offending and the gendered nature of sexual violence. *ACSSA Research Summary.* Retrieved from https://aifs.gov.au/publications/exception-proves-rule

Stoltenborgh, M., van Ijzendoorn, M. H., Euser, E. M., & Bakermans-Kranenburg, M. J. (2011). A global perspective on child sexual abuse: Meta-analysis of prevalence around the world. *Child Maltreatment, 16*(2), 79–101. doi:10.1177/1077559511403920

Stroud, D. D., Martens, S. L., & Barker, J. (2000). Criminal investigation of child sexual abuse: A comparison of cases referred to the prosecutor to those not referred. *Child Abuse & Neglect, 24*(5), 689–700. doi:10.1016/s0145-2134(00)00131-9

Tseris, E. J. (2013). Trauma theory without feminism? Evaluating contemporary understandings of traumatized women. *Affilia, 28*(2), 153–164. doi:10.1177/0886109913485707

Wade, A. (1997). Small acts of living: Everyday resistance to violence and other forms of oppression. *Contemporary Family Therapy,* 19(1), 23–39.

White, M. (2007). *Maps of Narrative Practice.* New York: WW Norton and Co.

White, M., & Epston, D. (1989). *Literate Means to Therapeutic Ends.* Adelaide: Dulwich Centre Publications.

World Health Organization. (1999). *Report of the Consultation on Child Abuse Prevention, WHO, Geneva, 29–31 March 1999.* Retrieved from Geneva: http://apps.who.int/iris/handle/10665/65900

Chapter 2

# The victim-centred family approach

## Introduction

This chapter provides an overview of the victim-centred family approach that was developed and refined over 25 years' practice at Cedar Cottage. We begin by presenting the underlying principles that inform the work before discussing the ways in which these are translated into the therapeutic approach outlined in this book.

This is followed by a discussion of the core dynamics of child sexual assault – secrecy, responsibility, protection/loyalty and resistance – that provide a useful framework for understanding the connections between the harming father's tactics of abuse and the impacts on the victimized child and other family members. They provide ideas for working with individuals and dyads in ways that enable family members to understand their experiences and the experiences of others in new ways. This opens up new possibilities for action and for relationships, for example, in overcoming the division sewn by the harming father between the victimized child and their mother and siblings.

The chapter concludes with a summary of the findings of a series of research studies of the Cedar Cottage Program. In addition to findings about rates of re-offending, it provides information about the nature and severity of the sexual abuse, the victimized children and about some other important outcomes of the program.

## The victim-centred family approach

### Integrated treatment

As outlined in the opening chapter, the therapeutic approach described in this book involves work with all members of the family but in a very different way from earlier family therapy approaches that inappropriately placed responsibility for the abuse onto mothers and victimized children and whose primary aim was to reunify the family. In contrast, the aims of the victim-centred family approach

## 18 The victim-centred family approach

are to end the abuse of the victimized child; to protect potential future victims; and to repair the harms done to the victimized child and all family members through the harming father taking and demonstrating responsibility for the abuse and its consequences. Co-developing, with mothers and other family members, ways of assessing whether the harming father demonstrates responsibility is a paradigm shift. In this way the harming father is not inadvertently placed at the centre of the recovery of others.

In order to achieve these aims the approach is an integrated one, in the sense that the work with the harming father is integrated with the work with the victimized child, her mother, siblings and extended family members. Integrated treatment, however, does not mean that the needs of all family members are treated equally: the victimized child is central and the needs of those harmed are privileged. The needs in relation to the harming father, in contrast, are responded to by invitations to act ethically and to face and demonstrate responsibility in ongoing ways.

### Principles underpinning the approach

Therapists working with families where a parent has sexually abused a child are faced with many competing needs and demands from both family members and other agencies. Holding a clearly articulated set of principles is essential to responding consistently and ethically to these demands. The competing, often contested understandings about the nature and effects of parental sexual assault also require therapeutic teams to develop shared understandings that contribute to decision making, which maintains a focus on the safety and well-being of the victimized child and others harmed by the abuse. The principles outlined below reflect such a shared understanding. They were developed over time by the Cedar Cottage team, were recorded as an *Ethos Statement*, and reviewed regularly as a standard against which practice could be critically evaluated.

### Safety of the victimized child, other family members and potential future victims remains at the centre of all intervention.

As will be seen in the examples provided in the book, the concept of safety for the victimized child is broad, encompassing not only physical but also emotional and psychological safety to redress her experiences of intrusion into all aspects of her life and relationships by the harming parent.

### The needs of the victimized child must prevail in any decision making.

Examples of the complexities of acting consistently with this principle are seen in decisions about the harming father's proposed access to the family home and contact with family members. The harming father is required to leave the family home and for many men the solution is to move back to live with their parents. This potentially interrupts the victimized child's and siblings' relationship with their grandparents. In order to prioritize the child's needs to maintain significant family relationships, harming fathers were not permitted to live with their parents.

### The non-offending mother is never to blame.

The mother has also been victimized and deceived but her experience of the abuse has often been invisible to her. The tactics to which she has been subjected need to be uncovered. This is essential to her own, her daughter's, and the family's recovery.

### It is possible to work with the whole family without sacrificing the needs of the victimized child.

It is not only the identified victimized child of any direct abuse who is harmed; the whole family is harmed by the actions of the harming father.

### Intervention is most effective when the perspectives of all family members are understood and each family member is able to see the perspective of others.

It has been in the harming father's interest to shape family members' perceptions of each other in ways that obscure his abuse and divide the victimized child from mother and siblings.

### For recovery and healing, each victimized individual needs to come to a position where they can review what they have been subjected to; recognize what others have been subjected to; and understand how this frames each person's reactions to them.

Part of this experience is then being able to understand and respond to the actions of others through a shared understanding of the harming father's tactics to which each has been subjected.

### To assist the child's healing it is essential that the harming father takes responsibility for all aspects of his abuse.

This includes planning, setting up the situation for the abuse, undermining the child's relationship with the mother, targeting the child for abuse, distancing the child from others and maintaining secrecy.

## 20 The victim-centred family approach

*Treatment begins when the harming father commits to a formal agreement which includes being contained by clear boundaries.*

This is part of a commitment to being accountable for his actions and not intruding on the recovery of people he has harmed. The boundaries and other limitations which are put in place may be modified during the course of treatment.

*The acts of facing and demonstrating responsibility by the harming father are central to his recovery, and to the healing of other family members.*

It is essential that family members are aware of the standards of honesty and transparency that the harming father has set so that they can assess his claims to accepting responsibility and his efforts to make reparation against these.

*An external mandate is an important way to support the work through ensuring continued commitment by the harming father.*

Therapy alone is an inadequate response to this serious and damaging criminal behaviour.

## Translating principles into the foundations of a therapeutic approach

### A broad scope for therapy

A key tenet of this approach is that a parent's sexually abusive actions are not isolated aspects of himself as a person, although he will typically assert this at the beginning of therapy. The whole range of his beliefs, attitudes, thoughts, feelings and behaviours must be reviewed in the light of standards of responsibility, accountability, respect for others and awareness of how his actions have affected, and continue to affect, others.

This requires his preparedness to explore all aspects of his personal history: his thoughts, feelings and actions and interactions with significant people in his life, both past and present. An important part of his thoughts that must be identified and addressed are the 'thinking errors' or 'cognitive distortions' which have enabled him to sexually abuse a child. For example he may have developed and hold the belief that the child must have wanted the sexual abuse to occur as she did not object. Another area of exploration is the origin and nature of his attitudes towards women and children, including his beliefs about what 'being a man' in our society means. Therapy at times may feel intrusive as a detailed examination of all aspects of a person's life is essential.

### The importance of external controls

Child sexual abuse involves a severe betrayal of trust and abuse of power. A parent who has sexually abused a child in his care has demonstrated by his actions that he does not honour the trust others had in him, and that he does not exercise power in a responsible and caring way. Therefore external controls are necessary, which include court mandated treatment and restrictions on his lifestyle and activities. We propose that community treatment of harming fathers should always be conducted with the oversight of a court responsible for criminal sentencing, as we do not propose treatment as a form of decriminalization. An alternative in some jurisdictions may be a child protection agency. Statutory bodies bring independence, scrutiny, public accountability and transparency, which are the antithesis of child sexual offending that is conducted in secret and through tactics designed to avoid accountability. Without a court mandate there is a significant likelihood that men in treatment will lack the necessary motivation to remain in treatment. Alongside this is the risk of men engaging in therapy to disarm and quell the anger of the mother of a harmed child, only to discontinue once the initial crisis has passed.

Restrictions on the harming father, such as barring him from the family home and from contact with the victimized child or any other children, provide the space and time away from his presence and influence that are required for the victimized child and other family members to recover from the harm he has inflicted.

### Demonstrating responsibility

The men who participated in the Cedar Cottage Program commonly asserted that they did not *intend* to harm their child/children. However, all were aware that their actions were wrong and likely to cause harm. An important issue for therapy is how they distanced themselves from acknowledging the harm they have caused. Facing the reality that they have harmed children is difficult but demonstrating responsibility for this and acknowledging their actions carries the opportunity to help the victimized child. It also creates hope for the men and can contribute to the development of a sense of self-respect and integrity. Harming fathers are invited to demonstrate personal responsibility in many ways. This includes through how they participate in the therapeutic process; their willingness to question and evaluate themselves; and adopting a committed position of being accountable.

### Life-long risk of re-offending

Men who have sexually abused a child are never 'cured'. They are considered to remain at risk of re-offending for the rest of their lives. To protect children, harming fathers should continue in maintenance therapy after the completion

## 22 The victim-centred family approach

of legally mandated treatment. Safety planning is the key to not re-offending (further explored in Chapter 9). Staying safe is also dependent on the harming father's awareness of the full impact of his behaviour on others; ability to self-evaluate on standards of responsibility; demonstration of a clear understanding of the thoughts, feelings and actions leading to his sexually abusing; and breaking down secrecy through facing up to significant people in his life and the lives of the children he has harmed.

### A different approach to the therapeutic relationship

Therapists base their relationship with harming fathers on a principle of respect for the stance these parents take to stop sexually abusing; to assist the recovery of the victimized child; and to review their lifestyle. Unlike therapy in other contexts and with other family members, trust is not a given in light of the serious breach of trust that lies at the heart of issues to be addressed in the harming father's treatment (Jenkins, 1990).

Contents of therapy sessions are confidential except where matters are disclosed regarding harm or risk of harm to others. This is referred to as limited confidentiality. Privacy is promoted but secrecy is not tolerated. Therapists must be aware of the risks of collusion with respect to information which needs to be shared or ideas and beliefs which support the victimization of others.

### Teamwork

The preferred structure for delivering an integrated response is a therapeutic team as it is unlikely that a single therapist can meet the needs of all family members. A victimized child is not safe if her therapist is also the therapist for the harming father. Similarly, the mother needs support to recognize and work through her responses to her partner's sexual abuse of their child and his treatment of her, the mother. If strong collaboration can be established, it is possible for the primary therapy for the victimized child or mother to be provided by another agency.

Teamwork takes many forms and addresses the potential risk of therapists being influenced by the harming father's attempts to build support for his views, wishes and demands. Much of the assessment and individual therapy with harming fathers should be undertaken with co-therapists viewing live through a one-way screen, or being in the room. Therapy with children and mothers should not generally be observed in this way. Conjoint work is conducted with therapists in the room together, though there may be therapeutic advantage in some circumstances to work with the parent dyad using a one-way screen. Those circumstances are typically relational sessions after there have been processes of acknowledgement by the harming father to the mother. Conduct of group therapy is a team process in planning, delivery and review, as is the regular assessment of progress of families through treatment.

The following vignette demonstrates some of the ways in which these principles are implemented in this therapeutic approach.

> Emma (11 years) and her sister Kate (8 years) were removed from their birth family due to physical abuse and neglect. They had been fostered by Barbara and Matthew for over 6 years when Emma disclosed that Matthew had been sexually abusing her for approximately 3 years. Barbara and Matthew also have one adult daughter, Karen who has a partner and small child and lives nearby. The statutory child protection agency removed Emma and Kate immediately. Initially Matthew remained in the family home as there were no children there and Barbara wanted to try to work things out with him. As a result of Barbara's decision not to separate from Matthew, she was not allowed to have any contact with Emma or Kate. In addition, their daughter Karen stopped visiting due to her father's presence. She missed Emma and Kate, who also missed her and Barbara.
>
> While Matthew was able to acknowledge the complex relationships and changes in the family due to his sexual abuse of Emma, his decision to remain in the family home was interrupting the relationships of his wife, daughter, grandchild and foster children. A condition of his participation in the treatment program was that he left the family home. This led to Emma and Kate reconnecting with both Barbara and Karen. It also allowed Karen's family to feel comfortable visiting Barbara and for Barbara and Karen to jointly work through issues related to Matthew's abusive behaviour. It was not until Matthew moved out that Barbara was able to identify his influence and control over her, and to develop clarity about her expectations for Matthew to demonstrate responsibility. The restrictions were placed on Matthew, not the family, but they had a direct impact on family life and relationships. These changes and the family's ability to assess Matthew's responses supported every family member's recovery.

The subsequent chapters provide a more detailed look at the ways in which these principles are applied in therapy with individual family members, as well as in dyadic and family work. These principles rest on an understanding of four key dynamics which we understand to operate in all instances of child sexual abuse.

## Key dynamics in child sexual abuse

In Australia as in many similar countries, therapy with children who have experienced sexual abuse and with sexual offenders is typically conducted separately. Each field of practice is based in specialist research and practice, with little overlap. Working with families after the disclosure of incest requires a way of understanding that brings together both fields of knowledge and expertise. In this part of the chapter, we propose a framework for understanding child sexual abuse that highlights the connections between the tactics of the harming

## 24   The victim-centred family approach

father, the impacts of these on the victimized child and other family members, and the agency that victimized children exercise despite the constraining conditions imposed by the harming father. Understanding these connections provides a way of integrating the therapy of all family members to achieve the goals of accountability by the harming father, safety and autonomy of the abused child and restored relationships between mothers, victimized children and siblings.

The context for the sexual abuse of a child is the unequal power relationship between parents and children, nested within gendered inequality in the broader society, that endorses male entitlement and privilege. Most parents respond to the relative vulnerability of their children with care and with behaviours that nurture the child's development. In situations in which a father chooses to abuse this relationship of vulnerability and trust through the sexual assault of a child, some common patterns can be identified. These arise from the tactics that the harming father uses to create the conditions for the abuse, to hide it, and to escape accountability for the abuse and its effects on the victimized child and family relationships.

### Secrecy

Enforcing secrecy is essential to the harming father's efforts to evade detection and to maintain ongoing access to the child (or children). The intimate sphere of family life provides the harming father with detailed knowledge of the child and of family relationships that can be used to shape tactics, which create a web of silence and entrapment. Silencing tactics, such as threats of harm to the child and other family members, can be titrated over time in response to the child's development and to counter increasing resistance. Enforced secrecy builds a wall of entrapment around the victimized child because 'not telling' at the first instance of abuse is so contrary to societal expectations of 'true' instances of interpersonal violence. It undermines the mother–child relationship because the seeds of doubt about complicity of the child in the sexual behaviours are sewn through the harming father's silencing of the child.

### Responsibility

Shifting responsibility for his abuse onto others characterizes the modus operandi of the harming father. He may blame the child directly (e.g. 'I know you wanted this'), but more commonly the child's mother (e.g. 'I wouldn't need to do this if your mother wasn't so frigid/depressed/rejecting'). He typically also paints a picture of himself as a victim of forces outside of his control, such as alcohol, loneliness or work pressures. For the father, these tactics enable the evasion of accountability for his choice to sexually abuse a child; for the child, they encourage self-blame and shame which further entrench secrecy. Blaming the mother directly or promoting the child's belief that the mother must be aware of the abuse is an attack on the mother–child relationship and builds further protection from detection for the abuser, with potentially devastating effects on the mother–child relationship.

## Protection/loyalty

As a consequence of the harming father's tactics aimed at enforcing secrecy and misplacing responsibility for the abuse, children are burdened with a sense of responsibility for taking care of and protecting others. Children commonly believe that their silence is essential to keeping the family safe and intact, and ensuring their mother's and siblings' well-being. They may believe that through their sacrifice, they are protecting younger siblings from abuse, although this is often illusory as it is not uncommon for siblings to be unaware until adulthood that each has been sexually victimized, so powerful is the father's enforcement of secrecy. The harming father effectively demands that the child put loyalty to the family before their own safety and well-being.

## Resistance

Importantly, the tactics that the perpetrator employs to enforce secrecy, shift responsibility, and exploit the child's loyalty to the family, need to be understood as efforts to overcome and disable the child's resistance (Wade, 1997). As mentioned in the previous chapter, narrative therapy has been an important influence in the development of the Cedar Cottage Program. Exploring the ways in which people have resisted being overwhelmed by problems, including efforts to violate and oppress them, is core to narrative therapy (White, 2007). Response-based practices build on this tradition with explicit acknowledgement that victimized people always resist the oppression of violence and abuse, though 'The precise forms resistance takes depends upon the unique combination of dangers and opportunities that exist in any given situation' (Wade, 1997, p. 29). Given the power imbalance between children and parents, and the coexistence of child sexual abuse and domestic violence, it is unsurprising that most forms of resistance by children need to be indirect and subtle. This is so far from the stereotypical expectations about victim resistance, that they are rarely recognized as such. Rather than focussing on the effects of the abuse, therapeutic conversations, which focus on exploring the details and implications of their responses, put people in touch with their strengths and capabilities. This approach is consistent with feminist empowerment approaches to working with sexual assault.

## Dynamics at the societal level

The dynamics of secrecy, responsibility and protection/loyalty operate on multiple levels, beyond the immediate context of the family and the child. In fact, their salience lies in the ways in which they reflect dominant societal discourses about violence against women and children. For example, the operation of secrecy at societal level can be seen in the silence that prevailed about the prevalence of sexual abuse of children prior to its 'discovery' through the activism associated with second wave feminism.

Bolen (2003) provides an example of the way in which misplaced responsibility for child sexual abuse can be institutionalized through a comparison of the gender of child sexual assault offenders in two sets of data: national United States child protection data and prevalence data from retrospective surveys. She found that: '[W]hereas mothers commit only 0.6 per cent of all *retrospectively reported* parental abuse, they commit, either solely or with a co-offender, 53 per cent of all *identified* parental abuse' (p. 1337). This reflects child protection practices that hold women accountable for 'failure to protect' children from abuse. Practices such as these mutualize responsibility for the man's sexual abuse of a child, and grossly distort the responsibility for men's abuse of children within families.

Dynamics of protection can be seen in professional responses to child sexual assault that resist working with the mother/child dyad in well-intentioned efforts to protect the child from negative interactions with their mother, when they are living day-to-day with the divisions sown by the perpetrator (Roberts, 1993). The framework for practice outlined in this book provides ways in which work with mothers and victimized children can assist them in developing an understanding of the divisive practices to which they have both been subjected.

Resistance can also be seen at the broader societal level in the feminist social movement that initially broke the societal silence about child sexual abuse and in more recent survivor movements that, for example, resulted in the establishment of a *Royal Commission into Institutional Responses to Child Sexual Abuse* in Australia. In addition to these broad social movements, 'everyday resistance' (Wade, 1997) needs to be integral to work of practitioners responding to intra-familial child sexual abuse, as they challenge practitioner and institutional responses that mutualize and minimize responsibility for the abuse and that shift blame onto abused children and non-offending mothers.

In each chapter of the book we unpack the operations of these common dynamics and explore the ways in which intervention can challenge secrecy, misplaced responsibility and exploited loyalty and honour and promote strength and resistance.

## The Cedar Cottage Program: participants, offences and outcomes

A comprehensive, retrospective study of the Cedar Cottage Program took as its sample all 214 men referred for assessment to Cedar Cottage between 1989 and 2003, of whom 93 were accepted for treatment. Data was obtained by reviewing and manually coding information in the program's clinical assessment and treatment files (Goodman-Delahunty, 2009; Goodman-Delahunty & O'Brien, 2014a and 2014b).

### Father–child relationship

Forty five per cent of the 214 men referred to the program between 1989 and 2003 were biological fathers and 55 per cent were non-biological fathers, i.e. step-fathers or the current partner of the child's mother. Biological and non-biological fathers were substantially similar on demographic features, characteristics of the index victim and index offence, as well as prior offending history. The child–offender relationship was also found to be unrelated to acceptance into treatment, treatment completion, and sexual reoffending (Titcomb, Goodman-Delahunty, & Waubert de Puiseau, 2012).

### Nature and severity of the sexual offending

The majority of men (82 per cent) referred to Cedar Cottage had been detected for victimizing one child. The balance of the men had been detected for victimizing between two and five children (13 per cent had victimized two children, 4 per cent had victimized three children; one man had victimized five children). Biological fathers were not more likely than non-biological fathers to have abused more than one child. Most victimized children were girls, with 91 per cent of harming fathers targeting girls exclusively. Similar proportions of harming fathers abused boys only (5 per cent), or both boys and girls (4 per cent).

The majority of harming fathers committed abuses against children under the age of ten years (59 per cent). Most of the youngest targeted victimized children were aged between five and nine years of age. However, three times as many biological as non-biological fathers abused children under the age of five years

The abuse perpetrated was severe: a clear majority of harming fathers had committed penetrative abuse (83.6 per cent), which included oral abuse by the harming father, oral penetration of the victimized child, digital penetration, and vaginal and anal intercourse (Goodman-Delahunty, 2014). The most common type of sexual abuse perpetrated by the fathers was sexual touching or fondling: nine out of ten committed this abusive act.

While it is often assumed that child sexual assault comprises a single impulsive act, and this is also the picture many harming fathers put forward when the assaults are discovered, this was not borne out by the experience of the program. The index offence of only 8 per cent of the harming fathers involved single occasions of a single sexual act with a child. More than half of the harming men (57 per cent) committed index offences that entailed between two and 50 separate incidents of abuse. Moreover, the average duration of the index offences was 3.5 years (range 0–16 years). In addition, on average, the offending parents engaged in multiple types of sexual acts with their children. In other words, a description of intra-familial offending as a one-off event was apt for fewer than 10 per cent of the sample (Goodman-Delahunty, 2014)

## 28 The victim-centred family approach

### A process for identifying additional victimized children

The way in which the assessment process was structured is an example of the program's primary focus on the protection of children. Men were not required to have made a statement or to have entered a plea in court to participate in the six to eight session assessment process. However, the men were clearly advised that any additional admissions were reportable under mandatory reporting processes. Nevertheless, all the men disclosed significantly more details regarding their offending behaviour during the assessment, including men who were not ultimately accepted into the program. Eleven per cent disclosed victimized children beyond the child or children identified in the index offence. They also provided additional details regarding the child's age when offending began, the duration and frequency of offending, the number of locations where abuse occurred, and the range and intrusiveness of abusive acts committed (Pratley & Goodman-Delahunty, 2011). This information contributed to the identification of previously undetected victims and enabled children to receive more effective assistance. Importantly for the field in general, the men disclosed more information about their offending than did the children they had assaulted, indicating that the extent and nature of abuse by harming fathers in the early stages of detection are often underestimated (Pratley & Goodman-Delahunty, 2011).

### Re-offending

Between 1989 and 2003, 56 per cent of the 214 men referred to the program were assessed as unsuitable and returned to court for sentencing. This 'treatment declined' group provided a comparison to the 'diversion' group for follow-up research to provide outcome data on the effectiveness of the Cedar Cottage model on the measure of re-offending.

In comparison with many other studies of recidivism, sexual re-offending was defined very broadly, that is, as any formal report to police involving contact and non-contact sexual re-offences against adults and extra-familial and intra-familial children. This reflects the recognized phenomenon in this field that police reports rather than arrest and conviction rates will capture with more accuracy the level of sexual reoffending (Butler, Goodman-Delahunty, & Lulham, 2012).

A sample of 208 harming fathers was followed up for an average of 9.1 years after their last contact with Cedar Cottage. In this period seven men who had been accepted into the program reoffended sexually (7.5 per cent), compared to 13 men who were declined entry to the program (16.5 per cent). Although these differences were not statistically significant, the time taken to sexually reoffend was longer in the diverted vs. the treatment declined group. The overall effect size for treatment was considered large (OR = 0.52, 95% CI = 0.18, 1.5), or in other words, treatment reduced the risk of reoffending by 50 per cent (Butler et al., 2012).

The authors of the study provided a detailed examination of the seven participants in the diversion group who sexually reoffended. Four had completed treatment, whereas three had been breached or withdrew before completion. Three of the four completers who sexually re-offended were referred to the Cedar Cottage Program in the first few years of its operation when the program was in its early stages of development and before legislative and regulatory amendments were implemented (Butler et al., 2012). These amendments allowed the program to return to court and seek approval to extend the treatment period by an additional year, for harming parents who had not made sufficient progress at the end of the two year mandated period. Of the seven sexual re-offences committed by program completers, four were non-contact offences, three were penetrative sexual re-offences, two by men who completed treatment in the first few years of the program operation, one by a non-completer. The overall recidivism data showed that in the 14 years between 1993 when the program introduced new provisions allowing harming parents to extend their treatment period, and the end of the follow-up period in 2007, no official police reports or convictions of any sexual offence against a minor were made regarding any of the 34 participants who completed treatment in the program (Butler et al., 2012).

## Other important findings from the program

### Reunification

There was a low rate of family reunification among the families who attended Cedar Cottage. A study of families who had completed at least 12 months of therapy found that less than a quarter expressed the intention to reunify (Case, 2008). It also found that for mothers, the disclosure of additional offences and/or victimized children significantly decreased interest in reunification, as did younger age of child at the time of abuse. Victimized children consistently reported low levels of interest in reunification at all stages of treatment. This indicates that the approach operated very differently from earlier family models where reunification was promoted as the goal of therapy.

### Preparedness to return men to court

When men who have committed serious child sexual assault criminal offences are offered treatment in the community, it is essential that treatment programs ensure that they comply with all treatment conditions. Ninety three men were accepted into the program during the study period. Of these, 53 (57 per cent) successfully completed the program. Forty (43 per cent) did not complete the program and returned to the court for sentencing. Participation of the majority of these men (32 of 40) was terminated by the program because they had breached the treatment agreement; the remaining eight withdrew voluntarily

## 30 The victim-centred family approach

from the program. This high rate of exclusion indicates that the Cedar Cottage Program took an ethical stance that prioritized child safety and adherence to standards on the part of harming fathers.

## Conclusion

The Cedar Cottage approach has a clear direction and set of principles, which guide the direction of intervention with all family members and assist with the complex ethical issues that arise in this work. Chief among these principles is safety – for the abused child, their siblings and mother, and future children with whom the man comes into contact. The outcomes from evaluative research attest to the capacity of the program for forging safety in this way.

This next four chapters focus on individual family members: harming fathers, mothers, victimized children and siblings. Each chapter outlines the experience of the harming father's tactics, the crisis of disclosure, and therapeutic work. The therapeutic processes are illustrated with brief vignettes based on synthesized cases and quotes from service users.

## References

Bolen, R. M. (2003). Nonoffending mothers of sexually abused children – A case of institutionalized sexism? *Violence Against Women, 9*(11), 1336–1366. doi:10.1177/1077801203256001

Butler, L., Goodman-Delahunty, J., & Lulham, R. (2012). Effectiveness of pretrial community-based diversion in reducing reoffending by adult intrafamilial child sex offenders. *Criminal Justice and Behavior, 39*(4), 493–513.

Case, D. (2008). *Reunification Interest in Families of Intrafamilial Abuse.* (Masters Thesis), University of New South Wales, Sydney.

Goodman-Delahunty, J. (2009). *The NSW Pre-Trial Diversion of Offenders (Child Sexual Assault) Program: An Evaluation of Treatment Outcomes.* Retrieved from https://www. researchgate.net/publication/298788143_The_NSW_Pre-trial_Diversion_of_Offen ders_Child_Sexual_Assault_Program_An_evaluation_of_treatment_outcomes

Goodman-Delahunty, J. (2014). Profiling parental child sex abuse. *Trends & Issues in Crime and Criminal Justice.* Retrieved from http://www.aic.gov.au/media_library/publications/tandi_pdf/tandi465.pdf

Goodman-Delahunty, J., & O'Brien, K. (2014a). Parental sexual offending: Managing risk through diversion. *Trends & Issues in Crime and Criminal Justice.* Retrieved from http://www.aic.gov.au/publications/current%20series/tandi/481-500/tandi482.html

Goodman-Delahunty, J., & O'Brien, K. (2014b). Reoffence risk in intrafamilial child sex offenders. *Technical and Background Paper Series.* Retrieved from http://www.crim inologyresearchcouncil.gov.au/reports/201314.html#1011-44

Jenkins, A. (1990). *Invitations to Responsibility: The Therapeutic Engagement of Men who are Violent and Abusive.* Adelaide: South Australia Dulwich Centre Publications.

Pratley, J., & Goodman-Delahunty, J. (2011). Increased self-disclosure of offending by intrafamilial child sex offenders. *Sexual Abuse in Australia and New Zealand, 3*(1), 10–22.

Roberts, M. (1993). Don't leave mother in the waiting room. *Dulwich Centre Newsletter*, 2, 21–28.

Titcomb, C., Goodman-Delahunty, J., & Waubert de Puiseau, B. W. (2012). Pretrial diversion for intrafamilial child sexual offending: Does biological paternity matter? *Criminal Justice and Behavior*, 39(4), 552–570.

Wade, A. (1997). Small acts of living: Everyday resistance to violence and other forms of oppression. *Contemporary Family Therapy*, 19(1), 23–39.

White, M. (2007). *Maps of Narrative Practice*. New York: W. W. Norton and Company.

## Chapter 3

# Engaging the harming father

## Introduction

A key goal of therapy with harming fathers is that they support the recovery of the other family members, firstly by acknowledging their sexually abusive behaviours and making the tactics they used to establish and maintain the assaults transparent to the mother and other family members; and secondly by making restitution to those hurt by their actions. Unless the harming father's therapy supports that of the others affected, his therapeutic outcomes are impaired. This restorative approach takes the outcomes for the victimized child as headline, rather than those of the harming father.

## The crisis of disclosure

The moment of disclosure is feared but nevertheless anticipated by the harming father, who will typically have developed a strategy in preparation for this event. In anticipation that the child may tell, he may have directly threatened the child or others close to the child. He may threaten the child with violence or predict a negative outcome for the child, including that she will not be believed and may be (further) distanced from the family, her mother in particular. If he anticipates that the child will be believed, the harming father may tell the child that he may go to prison, the family may lose their home, and that all the children may have to change schools. The child is burdened by the message that she will be responsible for the negative consequences for the family if she tells. The primary objective of the harming father is self-protection, which involves both silencing the child and insulating himself emotionally and psychologically from recognizing the harm caused by his actions.

Only after disclosure or discovery of the abuse does the extent of strategic conduct by the harming father in setting up, maintaining and acting to prevent or limit disclosure become visible. Our experience in work with harming fathers is that this strategic conduct does not stop at disclosure, and in fact it may intensify: 'That's not who I am. You know me. And that's just not who I am!'

> Bryce and Ruth had been together for eight years. They have one daughter and Ruth has two daughters from a previous relationship. Bryce sexually abused the elder of these two, Ebony aged 12. Bryce and Ruth ran a small business which at the time of disclosure was not doing well with debts rising and income declining. They worked long hours over mostly different time periods and on different tasks. It was while Ruth was working that Bryce would sexually abuse Ebony. Bryce never denied his abuse of Ebony after it was discovered. He constantly expressed regret, apologised and began spending all his time with Ruth. He saw an offer from a hotel chain and said he acted spontaneously to pre-purchase a number of weekend retreats for himself and Ruth. He began expressing his love for her frequently and started buying her flowers regularly as he had done early in their relationship.

Desperate to distance himself from being experienced or perceived as an abuser, the harming father may change behaviour after discovery by becoming closely attentive to his partner's apparent needs. The use of the term *apparent* is deliberate as this attentiveness usually includes expressions of reassurance, care and concern. It rarely extends to providing her with the details of his abusive behaviour, how this was executed or addresses consequences for other relationships such as that between the mother and victimized child. Through his actions, he attempts to influence her understanding of what this disclosure means. His behaviours are akin to courtship behaviours: giving gifts, sending caring messages or increasing personal contact such as calling often to ask after her and asking if there is anything he can do to help her. Through actions such as these, the harming father places the onus on the mother to be responsible to communicate what she is doing, how she is feeling and how she is managing both in relation to parenting and the status of the parental relationship. At the same time the harming father adopts the caring position of one who is willing to help. In these ways the harming father removes opportunities for the mother to process the impact of finding out about the assaults, with the harming father ever present and working hard to 'support' her.

> Jeff had sexually abused his and Kay's two eldest daughters. The eldest had moved from the family home soon after disclosure, as she and Kay were not able to speak about the abuse. Jeff had moved out (as required by Police and CPS) but regularly met Kay for dinner at a restaurant. This was something they rarely did after having children some 15 years earlier. One night while at a restaurant with Jeff, Kay looked around at other couples and loudly said 'Look at all these people. They look happy. I wonder how many of these men have sexually abused their children.' Jeff, embarrassed and flustered, paid the bill and they left. They went to Jeff's apartment and argued. Kay, who had not been drinking,

## 34  Engaging the harming father

> smashed some items and tried to hit Jeff. Jeff later reported to his therapist that he remained as calm as he could and drove Kay to where she had parked her car (he was not allowed near the family home). Jeff presented Kay's behaviour as irrational but something he understood. Kay was furious that Jeff seemed to be the one who was claiming to be 'reasonable'. In effect Jeff was preventing Kay from being able to process her feelings about his assaults. While taken by surprise by Kay's actions at the restaurant and subsequently, he relatively quickly characterized her behaviour as emotional and irrational. He inferred that Kay was 'mad or has something wrong with her' in contrast to his own 'rational and responsible' conduct during the evening

### Getting to the 'why?'

When parental sexual abuse is disclosed and confirmed it is predictable that the first question put to the harming father is: 'Why?' and in addition perhaps: 'What happened and how?' Volumes have been written in an effort to explain why adults sexually abuse children and more specifically how a parent could act this way. To date there is no consensus. Alan Jenkins (1990) observed the futility of searching for explanations of gendered violence as these are generally short on detail and likely to attribute responsibility for the behaviour externally from the person using violence. The two vignettes above present harming fathers who appear to be admitting to their sexually abusive behaviours. Rather than acknowledgement, the core feature of their responses is efforts to continue to control others, paired with minimization, which is a form of denial.

Early explanations offered by harming fathers commonly include statements in which the sexual offences are referred to using language such as *what happened* or *something that occurred*, examples of language describing actions with indeterminate agency (Lamb, 1991) that function to relieve the harming father of responsibility. Others closely associated with the harming father, including professionals responding to members of the family, may also adopt this type of language, which fails to attribute responsibility to the harming father. This can be quite subtle, such as a reference to *incidents* of abuse, but nevertheless this use of language serves to distance the harming father from responsibility. Describing what has been a process and experience of harm over an extended period of time as a series of abuse *events* or *incidents*, is a form of minimization that obscures the true nature of the sexual abuse. It sets up a platform to minimize acknowledgement of the impact of the sexual abuse, particularly the ongoing effects. All of these ways of talking can be understood as minimization, which reflects multiple layers of denial: of responsibility, seriousness, frequency, intent, location, level of intrusiveness, duration, the words used, impact of actions and much more.

> Steve (Mr A) arrived on referral to the program with a letter from his treating psychiatrist, who stated in part: 'Mr A's sexual conduct towards his step-daughter was out of character. It occurred in the context of Mr A experiencing significant stress at his place of work and on the day in question he had consumed half a bottle of whisky and in excess of the recommended dose of paracetamol.' Mr A had raped his 13 year old step-daughter after the family returned home from a Mother's Day Picnic.

This treating professional unquestioningly adopted the explanation which Steve was promoting. Jenkins suggests that a logical test of an explanation is to identify what the explanation implies as the solution or preventive measure. For Steve, it would be to address his work-related stress and to avoid the excess consumption of alcohol and paracetamol (possibly applying public health warnings on these products). An explanation can also be considered in relation to whether it attributes responsibility for the sexual abuse to the harming father or elsewhere. In parental sexual abuse it is common for marital stress or conflict to be offered as part of an explanation, which suggests the harming father's partner or ex-partner is at least partly responsible. This was in fact a tenet of earlier family therapy programs as outlined in Chapter 1.

## Tactics

Even when presented as 'impulsive', the conduct of harming fathers is strategic and detailed. When the Cedar Cottage Program was being established, relatively little had been written about how adults establish and maintain the sexual abuse of children, and even less on parents who sexually abuse. From the late 1980s several significant publications documented the planned, deliberate process by which assaults on children are typically conducted (Berliner & Conte, 1990; Christiansen & Blake, 1990; Conte, Wolf, & Smith, 1989; Haynes-Seman & Krugman, 1989; Lang & Frenzel, 1988).

Based on this body of literature, the process of initiating child sexual abuse became widely described as *grooming*, and in some jurisdictions grooming has become a separate sexual offence. Christianson and Blake (1990) have described grooming as a process by which the adult who holds or establishes a position of authority and/or trust, develops a close relationship with the child, gradually violating emotional and physical boundaries between themselves and the child, and finally entrapping them in secrecy. The initial concept of grooming the child did not fully encompass the actions of the offending adult and subsequently grooming has come to be understood as a broader process that also targets those in the child's world such as mothers and siblings, and extra-familial people such as teachers, neighbours, clergy, child protection workers and investigators (O'Leary, Koh, & Dare, 2017).

In an early group therapy session for harming fathers at Cedar Cottage the concept of grooming was introduced and the 12 men were asked to brainstorm the grooming strategies they used to set up, carry out or cover up and prevent disclosure of their sexual abuse of their children. Only a small list of behaviours was generated, confirming team members' idea that 'grooming' was an incomplete concept and that the concept of *tactics* may more accurately capture the complex and strategic behaviours that the men employed.

In the same group session the men were asked to consider the idea of *tactics* and the men identified a list of close to 100 behaviours and strategies they had used. A senior clinician at Cedar Cottage, Beatriz Reid, undertook a doctoral study exploring tactics used by perpetrators of intra-familial child sexual assault (Reid, 1998). One of the first to articulate the extent of these practices, Reid defined tactics as: 'Patterns of words and actions that the offender uses to perpetrate the abuse, and to set and maintain the context for the abuse' (p. 209).

The concept of tactics provides a more complete framework to understand the breadth, depth and impact of actions of the harming father. Reid identified that not only were the harming father's tactics identifiable in planning, preparing, engaging and preventing discovery or rebutting disclosure; the offender continues to use tactics in other contexts, including in the therapy room when addressing his sexual abuse behaviours.

Typically, tactics evolve over the course of assaults. Tactics are often graduated through the set-up, establishment, maintenance and post-discovery period, as well as in accommodation to the child's developmental stages. The following commonly used tactics are presented in order of the frequency of their use by harming fathers based on our experience at Cedar Cottage.

### Extortion

The use of bribery is widely reported as a tactic used to gain compliance or ensure silence about the abuse through the provision of money, privileges, alcohol, drugs, gifts and the like. We regard bribery as an unhelpful description as it does not align with the offender taking 100 per cent responsibility for the assaults, nor does it accurately describe the experience of the child. Bribery comprises corrupt conduct between two parties, who are, though rarely equal, each corrupt to differing degrees. Bribery implies a child is strategic, calculating and choosing to participate in a corrupt transaction. That is, whilst being the lesser party in a corrupt transaction, the child by accepting the 'bribe' is also culpable. A more accurate description is *extortion*. This term underlines the power differential and ways the child is compelled to comply with the harming father's demands. It more powerfully and accurately describes the process to which the child has been subjected. Often harming fathers and sometimes other family members have struggled with the term extortion as it directly confronts the image that the harming father has promoted of himself and equally the negative image of the child he has likewise promulgated.

## Use of force/violence

The use of force is underreported. In relation to young and dependent children, force is often not required to initiate sexual abuse but is more likely at a later stage when the harming father senses the child may tell and the abuse is about to end (the 'amelioration phase' described by Christianson and Blake (1990: p. 97)). In circumstances where the child lives with domestic violence, the child has ominous, direct experience of the level of violence of which the harming father is capable (Bancroft, Silverman, & Ritchie, 2012). In some circumstances the use of force can be a threat to hurt another family member or pet. In one case a father who was a firearms enthusiast and made his own ammunition demonstrated to his daughter how destructive his ammunition could be. In another case a step-father driving alone with his step-daughter in a rural location commented that it would be easy to dispose of a body and that it would never be found.

## Sexual arousal of the child

Achieving a sexual outcome is the primary outcome sought by the harming father. This is not limited to his sexual arousal and gratification but commonly also includes an interest in sexual arousal of the child. This is used by the harming father to prevent the psychological and emotional distress he may otherwise experience and to instil in the child confirmation of her culpability.

> While being touched sexually Rose was regularly asked by her father Eddie: 'How does that feel?' 'Are you OK?' 'Tell me when you're coming'

Eddie needs to convince himself that: 'I'm not hurting Rose' and that she is also enjoying 'being sexual' with him. Rose's responses, verbal and physical, provided evidence to him that he cares for her, *they* know what *they* (his belief of co-responsibility) are doing is wrong, but after all (in his mind), he asked Rose if she was OK and he would have stopped or changed what he was doing if she was not OK, and let him know. This way of talking with Rose constitutes further forced intrusion. Eddie's sexual touching of Rose elicits a physical, sexual response by her body. He compels her to describe it to him, provides her with a false sense of choice and tells her what her body's responses mean. The sexual abuse included Rose's first experience of arousal to orgasm, trapping her within a set of beliefs constructed by Eddie's attributing positive meaning to the behaviour and endowing Rose with a strong sense of culpability. Due to a strong sense of shame created by this culpability trap Rose is unlikely to describe Eddie's discussions with her in her initial disclosure. If Eddie were to acknowledge his sexual abuse of Rose, his first response is likely to be that he did not harm her. After all, he reasons, he checked with her and would have

## 38 Engaging the harming father

stopped if she had asked him to. This construction once again conveys mutuality; this was something they did *together*.

### Favouritism vs. alienation and deprivation

Tactics are matched to what the harming fathers assesses are the child's specific context or personal vulnerabilities. Accordingly a child may be subject to favouritism as she is conditioned to being sexually assaulted or she may be deprived of attention, with episodes of sexual assault imposed as a condition of limited access to the harming father or his approval. For example, two sisters seen at Cedar Cottage, unaware they were simultaneously being sexually abused, were divided by one being favoured and the other deprived of attention (while observing the 'special' favoured relationship her sister had with their father). Harming fathers also use gifts to denigrate and undermine the child's confidence and self-esteem, and to reinforce emotional deprivation. In another family, the father gave his two sons expensive gifts, and to his daughter whom he victimized sexually, he would give gifts such as a pair of socks or a hairbrush (Reid, 1998).

### Undermining the mother–child relationship

Directly undermining the mother's relationship with the child is common to almost all parental sexual abuse. This tactic ensures ongoing access to the child and to the greatest extent possible prevents the chance a child will disclose to her mother, and that if she does, she will not be believed. How this is achieved is explored in Chapters 4 and 5.

### Boundary violations

Boundary violations refer to harmful or potentially harmful breaches of physical and emotional space. These may comprise physical intrusions such as: entering the bathroom while the child is bathing or toileting; entering the child's bedroom while she is dressing/undressing; checking her bedding after she has gone to sleep; continuing to bathe and/or dry the child beyond an age of developmental necessity; applying medications or lotions to intimate parts of the child's body; or progressively touching a child more intimately in an effort to desensitize her to sexual contact.

> Terry removed the bedroom doors in the house, claiming that he wanted to emphasize a culture of an 'open family'. Family members, he said, needed to be comfortable with each other and have no shame about being naked or while engaging in all activities including personal care. He extended this to a policy of a 'no locked door' bathroom and removed the bathroom door when some of his children

> began locking it. The children had no privacy and were exposed to all behaviours in the house, including adult sexual behaviour.

Terry's action in removing doors is an extreme example of manipulation of the physical environment. 'No locked door' policy for bathrooms is a common tactic, as is shared bathing and use of bathrooms at the same time as children and adolescents. In cases where internal doors were removed, the harming father had recruited the mother to his stance as a philosophic and political position regarding family relationships.

> Troy paid particular attention to his daughter Myra's interest in music and fashion. He started listening to music by the same artists, buying tickets to concerts for them both. Robyn, Myra's mother was not interested in attending. One of the musicians Myra was interested in published photos of herself in sexual poses, clothed and unclothed. Troy purchased copies of these and used them to introduce explicitly sexual discussions with Myra, following which he sexually abused her over a period of four years.

Individuation is a developmental task in adolescence in which identity formation includes connecting to the known and familiar, as well as exploring difference, that is, elements external to family. The role of parents is to support adolescents to negotiate this space safely, but not join with them. Troy exploited Myra's steps towards individuation while distancing Myra and Robyn from each other. Rather than being distant and unavailable to protect Myra, Robyn was taking an appropriate developmental position as a parent, which Troy used and in the process undermined her relationship with Myra. As was the case for Myra, boundary violations are often used simultaneously with introduction of a sexualized environment.

### Sexualizing the environment

This includes: viewing sexually explicit online material, watching television or movies with sexual content, engaging in sexual talk through to exposing a child to adults engaging in sexual behaviours. This may include adults encouraging children to be comfortable with nudity of others or self. Nudity itself is not the problem. It is problematic when sexually motivated and includes efforts to influence a child to become comfortable with this, often against their own judgement. In the example above, the removal of internal doors in the family home affected privacy in use of bathrooms, removed a private space for dressing and sleeping as well as exposing children to the sexual behaviour of adults. This sexualizes the child's environment as well as facilitating boundary violations.

## Covert communication

Habituating a child to sexual abuse often involves specific cues or references to the behaviour which are only fully understood by the harming father and the child.

> Eric had a playful and outwardly good relationship with his daughter Naomi. He introduced sexual behaviour to her at a young age as a form of play and described it as *mucking around*. From that time on asking Naomi if she wanted to *muck around* or explaining what they were doing when absent from family was *mucking around*. This covert meaning was not discovered until nearly two years after disclosure when reconnecting Eric to family was being explored.

Covert communication is not limited to developing a language or code to cue sexual abuse. It can be used as a reminder of the consequences of telling or to reinforce dynamics set in play; for example, a look, a roll of the eyes, for the daughter to notice when her mother may be angry about something. Where the mother–daughter relationship has been actively undermined, a covert communication can reinforce the negative picture of the mother to the daughter, which the harming father has promoted. It can also take the appearance of an expression of care and support for the daughter while keeping its real intent, to control, out of vision.

### Other tactics

Harming fathers use myriad other tactics to establish and carry out sexual abuse as well as to prevent discovery or disclosure, including:

- Promoting a negative image of the child;
- Controlling the child in 'public' situations;
- Generally engaging in secrecy;
- Undermining the mother's agency (capacity to recognize and act);
- Ongoing reassessment of risk of discovery.

Central to all of these is the harming father developing a dominant script, the aim of which is to influence what people notice and more specifically how they perceive and experience each other and him.

## Tactics post-disclosure

The harming father reacts to discovery in a number of ways. Rarely is this to immediately and fully acknowledge his sexual abuse. Post-disclosure tactics are centred on self-protection by the harming father and reflect the tactics used in setting up and undertaking the sexual abuse. Recognizing the tactics or their relevance during the post-disclosure phase can help identify preceding tactics not yet identified and thereby assist in recovery of the victim and other family members, including the mother. The three common post-disclosure tactics are: i) denial; ii) attempts to communicate with the victim; and iii) efforts to influence others close to the victim. Each of these is discussed in turn.

## Denial

Denial may take several forms. It may be global, denying every part of a disclosure. Alternatively, it may involve minimization. For example, a harming father may acknowledge his actions but deny their intent, extent, significance or impact. Denial may relate to his responsibility for the sexual abuse, perhaps blaming intoxication or 'mistaken identity' of the victimized child. For example, one harming father who claimed mistaken identify told his partner, 'I thought it was you.'

## Attempts to communicate with the victim

After disclosure the harming father is likely to try to contact the child directly or influence someone else, usually a close family member, to do so. While it is less common today than 20 years ago for the harming father to attempt direct communication with the child, the possibility needs to be considered, particularly contact through social media.

## Efforts to influence others close to the victim

In most instances the harming father initially denies his sexual abuse to others close to the victimized child, as well as to statutory services. Many continue to deny. The denial is often elaborated upon by suggesting explanations, or inviting others into shared opinions of why the child may be making such – *allegedly false* – statements. This reaction is strategic and leverages off a dominant story that the harming father has developed regarding the child and their reliability. Consistent with previous tactics, the harming father continues to act in self-interest, though he typically presents as being concerned for the well-being of others in the family. He commonly raises doubts about the child's motivation, reliability and state of mind, implementing the tactics he has planned in anticipation of discovery.

---

**Useful therapeutic questions to elicit the tactics used:**

- Can you remember the when you first noticed C (the victimized child) in a sexual way? Did you see or imagine yourself being sexual with C from that moment?
- Do you remember the first time you sexually touched C or did something sexual while you were with her?

- How did you manage the risk of being caught or of C telling?
- How did you check whether you could touch her in intimate ways and keep her from telling?
- What did you say to her when you were doing sexual things to her?
- What did you say to C afterwards?
- How much thinking about C in a sexual way did you do between the first time you sexually abused her and the next time?
- Did you go to any special effort to check in on C after sexually abusing her? Not just immediately after but in the days and weeks which followed.
- Had you thought about what you would say if she told?
- How is it that P (your partner) doubted C's disclosure when she first found out?
- What sorts of things would you say about C to P before her disclosure? What was your response to P about C's disclosure?
- Is it possible to see part of what you did to protect yourself was to discredit C? Make people doubt her?
- What did you say to your parents when they found out?
- How had you talked about P and C to your parents before the disclosure?

## Tactics of the admitting offender

It is important to understand that a harming father is likely to conduct himself in strategic ways, even when he is 'admitting' that he has sexually abused his daughter. This is patterned and familiar behaviour centred on self-interest. 'Admissions' may be limited by different levels of denial. Some predictable themes include the following.

### Mutuality

This strategy is commonly used by harming step-fathers and involves the child or young person being portrayed as inappropriately interested in the step-father, who 'over-steps' or 'crosses the boundary'. This blurs or makes invisible the steps the adult in the relationship has taken to introduce the sexual behaviour and sets up the step-daughter to be viewed as an instigator, co-participant and competitor with her mother in relation to the harming step-father's attention. His claims of mutuality render his abusive actions almost invisible.

### Minimizing harm

Admitting offenders often suggest that the sexual behaviours were done in gentle and 'caring ways'. He may claim that the child was not hurt and that if at any time she had shown or expressed any discomfort, he would have ceased. This implies that the child was not harmed, the abuse consisted of misplaced care and that responsibility for preventing or stopping the abuse belonged to the child. However, in all of the cases at Cedar Cottage where the harming father asked the victimized child if she wanted him to stop and she said 'yes' or he promised 'this is the last time', the harming father resumed sexually abusing her at a later time.

## Re-igniting courtship with the mother

> Bryce's steps in moving closer to Ruth, to prove his commitment to her were taken without the knowledge of CPS or other services engaged with the family. The dominant story promoted by Bryce was that this was the couple's private business. Both Ruth and Bryce reported that spending time together was for the purpose of relationship renewal. Together they reflected on what had happened to them, framing it as having 'lost each other'. At a stage of disruption and uncertainty, along with intrusion into the family by external agencies, Ruth said she felt most secure with her closest confidant – Bryce.

As a result of Bryce's actions, Ruth is at risk of being assessed as a non-protective mother and agencies probably have some concerns about her mental health or capacity to function 'as she should'. Absent from this picture is clarity about Bryce's actions. Ebony, the victimized child, remains invisible.

Bryce's tactics include secrecy, isolation of Ruth and family and a focus on himself and his definition of Ruth's needs – as a wife to him, but not as a mother or as a woman. In providing levels of relief and attending to Ruth intimately and directly, Bryce interrupts other priorities for Ruth, including being there for Ebony. It is typical for mothers to hold self-doubt and self-blame. When she and Bryce 'rediscover' each other, it reinforces Ruth's belief that she is partly responsible, as this is a relational explanation. Several critical elements are missing from Bryce's actions: clear acknowledgement of his actions in planning and carrying out his sexual abuse of Ebony; clarity about Ebony's experience of being exploited and sexually abused; and space for Ruth to face the reality of Bryce's betrayal.

## Explicit and implicit explanations

Reigniting courtship with the child's mother is a self-protective strategy by the harming father. The implicit message is that the problem was co-developed and therefore has shared solutions. Embedded in this process of 'rediscovering' the relationship is the implication that the child's mother was unavailable (sexually) to the harming father and had she been available, he would not have sexually abused their daughter. Maternal sexual unavailability is frequently cited by harming fathers as a reason to 'turn to a daughter' and is sometimes adopted as an explanation by professionals (Ward, 2002). Underlying this view is that men need sex and if wives do not provide it their male partners may turn to their children for sex. There are many variations around this theme and one of the more subtle is when the harming father has presented to the extended family over a period of time (sometimes years) that his wife is 'hard work'. Undermining and denigrating her in the eyes of his family prepares the groundwork for others to 'understand' his actions.

It is often unnecessary for others to suggest maternal culpability, as women commonly blame themselves. If they acquiesce to the harming father's courtship and become 'available' they may inadvertently confirm for themselves and their partners that they are at least in part to blame. This perspective may not be limited to beliefs about availability for sexual contact, but extend to not being available *enough* or at the *times* he wanted sex or in the *ways* he wanted to have sex. At times harming fathers have expressed dissatisfaction and denigrated their partners for their physical appearance, including changes to their bodies in the years following childbirth. Each of these actions and beliefs centre upon core misconceptions about male sexuality, including expectations that women have a role of servicing men's sexual 'needs'.

> **Therapeutic questions to identify the limitations of his admission may include:**
>
> - What are you saying about C (victimized child) if you are saying this was something you did together, rather than what you initiated?
> - What difference might it make for P (partner) to understand exactly how you initiated the sexual contact? What might be the implications for her responding to C if she knows this?
> - Is this the right time for you to be spending time alone with P? Asking her to meet over dinner? Could it be confusing for her if it's like a date?
> - How tempted are you to work hard to get P to understand your point of view?
> - What loyalties might P be juggling at this time?

### Misunderstanding tactics and inadvertent attribution of power to the harming father

The actions used to groom a child for sexual abuse are common with all types of human interaction; it is the sexual intent which differentiates them as harmful. It is erroneous to think that harming fathers possess high-level capacities to control and manipulate others. They do not hold special powers and once their actions are made visible, this can be recognized. Perhaps the most troubling interactions are those involving covert communication, as they can take some time to identify. It is important for people supporting families to recognize there is nothing special about covert communication. We all do it. We have often demonstrated this in training sessions by posing the question:

Who here has not been in a social situation with a partner who has said or done something you don't approve of (or maybe you said or did something disapproved), and you have exchanged a look confirming the disapproval? Nobody else sees it but you both understand exactly what it means.

Contemplating covert communication paves the way to better understand the child's experience. The day-to-day experiences for abused children comprise systematic exclusion from family relationships, isolation and being controlled, not simply 'occasions' of sexual abuse.

## Engaging harming fathers in meaningful therapy

### Legislative support for engagement

The legal and social context of the harming father has critical significance to engagement in therapy. Presentation to counselling generally follows the harming father acknowledging their sexual abuse behaviour, in part at least, and doing this may risk legal and social (family) sanctions. In most jurisdictions admitting guilt for child sexual assault has substantial personal negative consequences. Sanctions include major losses: of liberty through imprisonment; of family relationships; of employment; and social connections. Legal systems generally provide little to encourage admission of guilt. Admissions are unlikely, unless the incentive for harming parents to address this behaviour and its consequences are established. Legal systems may provide for reduced sentences based on guilty pleas, but this may not be sufficient incentive in the pre-trial phase. The key incentive of the Cedar Cottage legislation was participation in a community-based program over two to three years in place of a custodial sentence. This is not available in all jurisdictions but is an example of a scheme in which the incentive to plead guilty and certainty of process were foundational in engagement of the harming parent.

Early engagement in therapy is best. Denial is less likely to become fixed or family members further harmed as a consequence of continuing narratives which conceal the harming father's actions. It is possible to engage the harming father after legal proceedings, but denials and justifications may have consolidated and the mother–child relationship may have deteriorated as a result. Early engagement in therapy by the harming father may also help others to believe and validate the child.

The legislation supporting the Cedar Cottage Program provided a number of incentives for early confirmation of sexual abuse by harming parents. First, a request by a harming parent for inclusion in the program was unable to be used as evidence of guilt or referred to in subsequent proceedings. The content of assessment interviews could not be used in prosecution if a parent chose to withdraw from assessment or was found to be unsuitable for the program,

## 46 Engaging the harming father

unless a harming parent who was assessed as unsuitable for the program later chose to raise issues about the assessment in court. Although these protections applied, the assessment had limited confidentiality, with disclosure of any additional child abuse reported to child protection authorities.

### *Therapeutic engagement*

The central tenet of engagement in this therapeutic approach is commitment to personal responsibility. In assessment the harming father is initially asked for biographical and personal details of himself and his family. Prior to discussing sexual abuse, he is provided an opportunity to take a personal position (a 'stand') regarding sexual abuse of children in general and then a position about abuse of his own child. This establishes a reference point from which he can review his own thoughts, feelings and beliefs as well as setting in place initial goals and standards against which he will be invited to review the written material that is required at different stages of the therapy.

Typically engagement involves the harming father setting goals of: taking full responsibility for his actions (though it is unlikely he is aware of the full meaning of this at this stage); wanting to understand and explain why he sexually abused; committing to take whatever steps are possible to help people he has hurt; and demonstrating that he will not sexually offend again. From the outset it is clear there is a struggle present for most harming fathers, between attending to the impact of their actions on others and self-interest. The harming father is asked to reflect on what may be restraining him from conducting himself in respectful and responsible ways, as well as identifying what it may take for him to overcome those restraints.

An absence of self-respect and low self-esteem are typical features of harming fathers at presentation. Taking steps towards responsibility is presented as an opportunity for them to not only achieve the goals they set for assisting others but also to regain self-respect. While a desire to be trusted, forgiven and accepted is strong, rebuilding self-respect has proven to be a highly motivating focus for engagement (Jenkins, 1990, 2009).

The most common initial goals and standards for harming fathers are to:

- Take responsibility for their child sexual assault;
- Address wherever possible the effects of the sexual assault;
- Develop a responsible explanation for their sexual assault which includes commitment to being safe, accountable and to desisting from re-offending.

The concept of standards is usually novel to the men entering therapy, so some examples are provided. The standards are used to assist the men develop practices of reflection and self-assessment of their current conduct. Common standards applied to these goals include:

Engaging the harming father   47

- Being honest, recognizing this applies to both acts and omissions;
- Ensuring others, victimized children and mothers in particular, are not left blamed or burdened in any way;
- Focussing on personal responsibility (often reflected in 'I' statements as opposed to use of 'we');
- Distinguishing excuses and explanation from statements in which responsibility is owned.

Early attempts by a harming father to explain sexual abuse behaviour are often highly theoretical, speculative or general and lack elements reflecting personal responsibility. They are influenced by personal, social, cultural and societal beliefs as well as denial, which is motivated by self-interest and an ego-centric view of the world. A more productive approach is for the man to detail what he did and how he went about, provided he is not restrained by factors such as shame, guilt, self-disgust or self-protection (White & Epston, 1989).

In the police and/or child protection investigation after discovery, the harming father is typically asked to respond to questions about his sexual assault behaviours. Rarely does he engage in a free narrative and this is a context in which he is generally cautious. If a rationale for personal responsibility is co-developed in therapy it is possible for him to detail what he did. In therapy, harming fathers come to understand how leaving it up to the child to detail the abuse is *unfairly* leaving them with the burden of telling. Furthermore the harming father begins to realize that it is unreasonable for him to acknowledge his conduct simply by attaching it to the child's disclosure and measuring his acknowledgment simply against the child's disclosure. It is *always* possible for the harming father to provide more detail than the child about the assault and related actions and preparations. Children's disclosures rarely contain details of the words used by the harming father, apart from specific threats or verbal coercion, usually related to specific events rather than conversations over time. When the harming father provides specific detail about his actions including words used, locations and times chosen, risk of discovery managed, a much richer description of the child's experience of the sexual assaults is revealed. This often uncovers further layers of coercion and entrapment.

**Useful questions for engaging harming fathers in therapy:**

- What did it take for you to admit guilt and seek assessment by this program?
- What is in it for the rest of your family for you to receive treatment?
- If you were harmed as a child yourself, can you also take responsibility for sexually abusing C?
- What risks are you taking in facing up?
- If P and C have been weighed down by the effects of what you have done, are you prepared to shift that to yourself wherever you can? To remove doubt and uncertainty by providing details of what you did?
- What do you think is important for P and C to know about your actions?

## 48 Engaging the harming father

Therapeutic work with those who sexually harm is confronting and sensitive. As outlined in Chapter 2, team work is the preferred approach to this work and essential when multiple family members are participating in therapy. This ensures that family members have an ally who is unambiguously aligned with their interests through the therapeutic process. The power dynamics, widespread and sustained use of tactics by those who harm suggest the merit of team work, even when a provider is working solely with harming fathers. This supports the transparency and reflexivity that is required in this work.

## Assessing risk and safe case management

Risk assessment is an important element in planning, supervision and case management. However, the limitations of risk assessment in parental child sexual abuse need to be understood. Risk assessment is focussed on risk of future re-offending, which is important. It does not, however, directly attend to the harm and continuing effects for child victims and others caused by past sexual offending. One of the differences between assaults by parents and other offenders is that, as outlined in Chapter 1, while harming parents are generally in the lowest risk group for re-offence, victims of parent–child sexual assault as a group have higher risk of severe and continuing effects.

The limitations of risk assessment tools currently in use need to be acknowledged. A number of researchers and theorists assert that, at best, the available risk assessment tools identify associations of a range of factors with re-offence, and the role of therapists is to apply knowledge of the associations to their therapeutic practice (Ward & Beech, 2015; Ward & Fortune, 2016). Contemporary risk assessment formulates risk through structured clinical judgement, which includes the use of formal risk assessment instruments. Risk factors overlap to some degree with therapeutic target areas associated with the relational effects of parent–child sexual assault. These include whether or not the harming father has addressed his own denial; his beliefs about his actions and their impact on others; the degree of his self-awareness and willingness to self-regulate; and his response to becoming accountable and subject to supervision by others (Hart et al., 2003). Formulating future risk also needs to consider protective factors, including the family environment, absence of domestic violence, how conflict is managed, strength of mother–child relationships, his beliefs about past sexual assaults, and whether he recognizes his potential to re-offend in the future.

Effective risk formulation and safe case management for families require details of dynamics of the child sexual assault to be known and understood by affected family members. For this reason, contact between the harming father and the child who was assaulted or her siblings is generally not recommended early in the therapeutic process.

Following the disclosure of sexual abuse by his step-daughter and before being assessed for treatment, Matthew formed a new relationship with Marie, a mother of two boys. Matthew had disclosed to Marie that he had sexually assaulted his step-daughter, however in a joint assessment interview with Matthew and Marie it became clear that he had not shared all the details of his sexual abuse-related behaviours. Omissions included his sexualization of the family environment. He described this detail as all 'in the past' and that he and Marie were committed to working through the program together, and doing 'whatever it takes'. He had convinced Marie that her boys were safe around him as he would not be living with her and because he had told her about his sexual assaults. He had also convinced her he could 'beat this (his sexual assault issue) with her support'. Marie argued that she did not need to know anything more than the bare details she had and believed he was genuine in wishing to not repeat the behaviour. She had closely observed him when with her and her sons and regarded him as safe. Marie was asked if she had thought about whether Matthew's previous partner would also have felt he was a safe person. She agreed with the proposition, but added that his previous partner should probably have noticed some 'signs', giving an indication that she had been recruited by Matthew into an account of the abuse in which he was shifting responsibility to his previous partner. Rather than challenge or contradict Marie's position of not needing to know more about the sexual assaults, the therapist conducting the assessment asked if Marie knew or was interested in how Matthew kept the sexual assaults secret, how he silenced his step-daughter and the ways he kept this from his previous partner and asserted influenced over her. Marie indicated that she did not know about this but would like to know. Matthew immediately tried to give brief answers on the spot while arguing the details were not important. The therapist told Marie that these questions were as much about Matthew as they were about his sexual assaults of his step-daughter. The inadequacy of Matthew's responses and position the therapist took were sufficient for Marie to indicate she would like to know more and have an opportunity to speak privately with a therapist. She accepted that until this happened, contact with her sons by Matthew could wait.

## Ethics of treatment and community supervision

Conducting a therapeutic program under legal mandate with men who have committed serious and harmful criminal offences raises many ethical issues. In fact most decisions confronting therapeutic staff involve complex ethical considerations as discussed in the following examples.

### *Admissibility of assessment material in court*

The first ethical principle for helping professionals is to do no harm, followed by respect for human rights and dignity, fidelity and responsibility, integrity

## 50 Engaging the harming father

and justice. Social and legal responses to child sexual assault are heavily weighted against victimized children being able to disclose, be believed and supported (Cossins, 2010). In developing integrated responses to intra-familial child sexual abuse, the principles of natural justice ('procedural fairness' in some jurisdictions) are applied in managing harming fathers. Child sexual abuse is characterized by inequality between the victim and person doing the sexual abuse. Attempting to re-balance the rights of children and parents who harm does not improve outcomes for children. Rather than balancing the rights of each person with each other, the primary shared interest should be the recovery of the child victim and the interests of others need to be framed around this. For example, the interests of the harming father should be inextricably linked to acknowledgement and supporting the safety and recovery of the child.

> Craig appealed a decision which assessed him as unsuitable for community-based treatment. During the assessment he had acknowledged his sexual behaviour and indicated he would plead guilty, but maintained that his daughter was 'sexually provocative' and 'promiscuous'. In his appeal he denied using these descriptions of his daughter. The Court found in favour of Craig, determining that the assessing therapist had been unduly influenced by these descriptions and that Craig's admission of guilt (*to engaging in sexual behaviours*) meant he should be re-assessed. In the subsequent re-assessment Craig made no reference to the assertions made in his first assessment of his daughter being sexually provocative.

This example identifies the challenges of providing treatment within the legal system, and raises ethical issues in relation to establishing a community treatment program for harming fathers. How are the rights of harming fathers to be regarded in relation to the rights of children harmed? How can adding to harm be avoided? Should children be given a choice about whether the parent who harmed them enters a treatment program? How can therapeutic work with the harming father prevent intrusion into the victim's life?

Craig's case led to procedural and legislative amendments. Assessment interviews were thereafter digitally recorded and conducted with a co-therapist. This meant harming parents could no longer deny statements they made during the assessment. In therapy, statements of this type can be explored for their meaning to the harming father and their influence on other's beliefs. For example, what was the impact on Craig's daughter of his assertion that she was 'sexually provocative and promiscuous'? While he stated that he was responsible for his actions in relation to engaging in sexual abuse of his daughter, he portrayed his daughter as partly responsible, without acknowledging that she may have been harmed by his characterizing of her as provocative.

The amended legislation included a preamble emphasizing the purpose of the legislations:

> The purpose of this Act is to provide for the protection of children who have been victims of sexual assault by a parent or a parent's spouse or de facto partner. The Act provides for the establishment of a program administered by the Department of Health. In the implementation of the Act, it is intended that the interests of a child victim are to prevail over those of a person pleading guilty to a charge of sexual assault in relation to the child.
>
> (s.2A, NSW Pre-trial Diversion of Offenders Act 1985)

This legislative amendment provided clarity regarding the purpose of the program and made explicit the aim of protecting of children; it removed the idea of balancing children's rights with those of harming parents.

### Children's role in the harming father's treatment

Perhaps the most central ethical concern in undertaking this work is to avoid victimized children being compelled to engage in conjoint processes with the harming father, or doing so, according to his schedule rather than their own. An often overwhelming 'family belief' is that the child will agree to reunification. Expectations such as this need to be articulated and placed alongside other expectations or goals, such as the need for the harming father to detail his offences, their impact on others and to demonstrate steps towards taking responsibility. Working through any conflicts of goals makes these processes visible and in doing this every family member is given opportunity to be heard and express their wishes.

### Access by siblings to the harming father

Ethical concerns attach to decision-making about siblings. Should the non-abused siblings of the victimized child be able to have continuing contact with the harming father? What restrictions should be placed on him in relation to places he can visit, with whom he can have contact and activities he can engage in? A clear focus on the impact on the victimized child and the sibling relationships should be the leading consideration in decision-making. This consideration is closely associated with the degree to which the father is taking responsibility for his actions.

### Disclosure of additional assaults and victims

The establishment of conditions for contact with siblings was associated with harming fathers not merely measuring their acknowledgements of sexual abuse

## 52 Engaging the harming father

behaviour against their children's disclosures (which is the usual response in most treatment programs); in addition, harming fathers disclosed more abusive behaviour in almost every case (Pratley & Goodman-Delahunty, 2011). An unforeseen ethical consideration arose where this included disclosure of newly identified victims. Disclosures in relation to children are without question subject to mandatory child protection reports. Most disclosures however related to sexual abuses committed during the harming father's adolescence, directed at their siblings or other close relatives, such as cousins. Where there had not been disclosure by those now adult survivors, the ethical issue was whether their lives should be disrupted through raising the abuse, perhaps risking their being re-traumatized. In these cases, the police were briefed about the context of the reported behaviour and initiated contact sensitively with the identified adults, with counselling support pre-arranged should it be necessary. Despite concerns that this may cause harm, every adult contacted expressed relief and gratitude. In one case two adults victimized as children wanted the harming father prosecuted. This happened and the man received a prison sentence to be served at the completion of his treatment program. Implications for extended family members are further explored in Chapter 8.

In relation to harming fathers, a committed approach to informed consent, for example, discussing implications of making further disclosures is anchored to the core program principle of the harming father demonstrating responsibility. It is characterized as strength to demonstrate responsibility in the full knowledge of consequences which may follow. From the perspective of the treatment provider it is a matter of ethical practice that all program participants are fully informed of these risks and are not left feeling misled or caught by surprise. Under the Cedar Cottage Program protocol further disclosures were the subject of mandatory reporting. If further offences were added to the prosecution and should harming fathers not enter or complete the program, they faced a longer period in prison. All program applicants were encouraged to disclose fully in assessment as only at that point in time could the offences be included in the diversion. Later disclosure did not automatically mean exclusion from the program but may attract additional sentencing.

> In assessment Terry indicated his sexual abuse of his daughter was more extensive than she had disclosed. Before providing details he asked what the implications of further admissions would be. Terry said he felt himself to be in a double bind. Having acknowledged there was more sexual offending, he needed to volunteer these details to access the program. However if he disclosed and did not enter the program or complete it, he faced a longer period of imprisonment. Terry was asked to consider the implications for his daughter of the decision he faced and he readily identified that it would be better for him to take responsibility for disclosing. He anticipated (correctly it as it eventuated) that his daughter felt most shame and embarrassment about the undisclosed sexual abuse and that he could attend to this

> by including this information in his disclosure. Some of the team undertaking the assessment were attracted to the idea Terry promoted that he had been placed in an unfair position. In helping Terry to address this, the team discussed Terry's process in reaching this point, the information he had been provided and the connection between his assessment and later treatment and his daughter's needs. The team concluded that Terry had not been entrapped. He asked to be diverted to treatment. He knew his sexual abuse of his daughter was more extensive than she disclosed. His assessment was for treatment, not to avoid negative consequences for his conduct. Further, his treatment was inextricably linked to acknowledgement of the full extent of sexual abuse of his daughter. Terry's description of himself being in a double bind was not a result of being unethically placed in a position of having to admit more offences. Rather, it was a moment of hesitation as he recognized the implications for him of disclosing more. Re-focussing him on his decision to assist his daughter's recovery resulted in Terry prioritizing taking responsibility for his conduct.

## Mothers who harm

In the history of Cedar Cottage only one woman was referred for treatment. The assessment did not proceed because the applicant was unwilling to agree with a treatment condition of living away from children. Our experience is therefore limited in this respect and this group of harming parents is covered in brief here.

The sexual abuse of children by women is extremely disturbing for a child and can lead to serious long-term effects (Denov, 2004; Stathopoulos, 2014). Some significant different dimensions compared to men who sexually abuse children include: prevalence; mental illness; significant trauma; and co-offending, which are discussed here.

There is now general consensus that female sex offending makes up a very small percentage of all sex offences (Horvath, Davidson, Grove-Hills, Gekoski, & Choak, 2014; Peter, 2009; Quadara, Nagy, Higgins, & Siegel, 2015; Stathopoulos, 2014) with prevalence data suggesting that women comprise three to ten per cent of those who sexually abuse children (Quadara et al., 2015). Prevalence estimates vary considerably however, with evidence in different reports of some *under-* reporting, but also *over-* counting when women judged to be 'failing to protect' who have not themselves abused a child, are counted as offenders (Bolen, 2003; Horvath et al., 2014). Diana Russell's (1986) large-scale, landmark study continues to yield some of the most comprehensive data on child sexual assault, collected through in-depth face-to-face interviews. Russell found a total of ten female incest offenders in a sample of 930 women. The perpetrators comprised one mother, sisters, cousins and more distant relatives (Russell, 1986). This scale and methodology have not been replicated so confirmation of current prevalence is not available.

## 54 Engaging the harming father

In considering other dimensions of female offending, it needs to be noted that small sample sizes in studies limit the conclusions able to be drawn. However one dimension on which the available evidence suggests that women differ from males who harm is in relation to mental health problems, which are disproportionately evident in females who sexually harm children (Wijkman, Bijleveld, & Hendriks, 2010). This may be particularly the case for women who sexually assault their own offspring. Analysis of the case files of five women who had sexually abused their own children, found all to have personality disorders (Grattaglianno et al., 2012 in Horvath et al., 2014). It seems likely that such disturbance may be the result of childhood abuse at the severe end of the spectrum, which is also found to be more common among females than males (Miller, 2013, Strickland, 2008, in Horvath et al., 2014).

A second difference between women and men who sexually abuse is that women are more likely to commit the acts in the company of another adult, most commonly males (Budd, Bierie, & Williams, 2017). In a Dutch study of all female sex offenders known to the criminal justice authorities over ten years, in almost two thirds of the 111 cases, the women had co-offended with a male (Wijkman et al., 2010). Budd et al. (2017) note that the literature identifies two types of female co-offenders: women who have been coerced by a male co-offender and those who participate willingly. Women acting alone or with other women were more likely to have abused boys, and children unknown to them, than women acting with a male co-offender (Budd et al., 2017).

Another distinction between male and female offenders suggested by the literature is that abuse by females is more likely to be a one-off event (70% vs 41%) (Russell, 1986). Females were also found in Russell's study to be younger than male incest offenders, 44 per cent being under 15 years of age, compared to 17 per cent of males (Russell, 1986). The evidence also suggests that women are more likely than male offenders to abuse younger children (Peter, 2009)

Unique treatment issues we identify for harming mothers include: particular issues of stigma or shame for harmed children abused by their mother; the likely lack of group work opportunities; and risk of minimization by other involved agencies.

## Conclusion

Work with harming fathers to address and prevent child sexual assault offending is complex and slow, and can involve redress to, as well as participation of, many family members and ideally a team response. There are myriad ethical challenges to be balanced. Yet this work also holds promise for forging enduring safety for harmed children, other family members and children who are yet to enter the lives of this individual.

## References

Bancroft, L., Silverman, J. G., & Ritchie, D. (2012). *The Batterer as Parent: Addressing the Impact of Domestic Violence on Family Dynamics* (2nd ed.). Thousand Oaks, CA: Sage.

Berliner, L., & Conte, J. R. (1990). The process of victimization: The victims' perspective. *Child Abuse and Neglect*, 14, 29–40.

Bolen, R. M. (2003). Nonoffending mothers of sexually abused children – A case of institutionalized sexism? *Violence Against Women, 9*(11), 1336–1366. doi:10.1177/1077801203256001

Budd, K., Bierie, D., & Williams, K. (2017). Deconstructing incidents of female perpetrated sex crimes: Comparing female sexual offender groupings. *Sexual Abuse: A Journal of Research and Treatment*, 29, 267–290.

Christiansen, J. R., & Blake, R. H. (1990). The grooming process in father–daughter incest. In A. L. Horton (Ed.), *The Incest Perpetrator: A Family Member No One Wants to Treat* (pp. 88–98). Thousand Oaks, CA: Sage Publications.

Conte, J. R., Wolf, S., & Smith, T. (1989). What sexual offenders tell us about prevention strategies. *Child Abuse & Neglect*, 13(2), 293–301.

Cossins, A. (2010). Alternative models for prosecuting child sex offences in Australia. Retrieved from http://www.law.unsw.edu.au/sites/law.unsw.edu.au/files/docs/na tionalcsareformcommitteereport2010.pdf

Denov, M. S. (2004). The long-term effects of child sexual abuse by female perpetrators: A qualitative study of male and female victims. *Journal of Interpersonal Violence*, 19(10), 1137–1156.

Hart, S. D., Kropp, P. R., Laws, D. R., Klaver, J., Logan, C., & Watt, K. A. (2003). *The Risk for Sexual Violence Protocol (RSVP): Structured Professional Guidelines for Assessing Risk of Sexual Violence*. British Columbia, Canada: Mental Health, Law and Policy Institute, Simon Fraser University.

Haynes-Seman, C., & Krugman, R. D. (1989). Sexualized attention: Normal interaction or precursor to sexual abuse? *American Journal of Orthopsychiatry*, 59(2), 238–245.

Horvath, M., Davidson, J., Grove-Hills, J., Gekoski, A., & Choak, C. (2014). It's a lonely journey: A rapid evidence assessment on intrafamilial child sexual abuse. Retrieved from London, UK: http://eprints.mdx.ac.uk/13688/1/Its%20a%20lonely %20journey_final%20%282014%29.pdf

Jenkins, A. (1990). *Invitations to Responsibility: The Therapeutic Engagement of Men who are Violent and Abusive*. Adelaide, South Australia: Dulwich Centre Publications.

Jenkins, A. (2009). *Becoming Ethical: A Parallel, Political Journey with Men Who Have Abused*. Dorset, UK: Russell House.

Lamb, S. (1991). Acts without agents: An analysis of linguistic avoidance in journal articles on men who batter women. *American Journal of Orthopsychiatry*, 61(2), 250–257.

Lang, R. A., & Frenzel, R. R. (1988). How sex offenders lure children. *Sexual Abuse: A Journal of Research and Treatment*, 1(2), 303–317.

O'Leary, P., Koh, E., & Dare, A. (2017). *Grooming and Child Sexual Abuse in Institutional Contexts*. Retrieved from Sydney: https://www.childabuseroyalcommission.gov.au/ sites/default/files/file-list/Research%20Report%20-%20Grooming%20and%20child% 20sexual%20abuse%20in%20institutional%20contexts%20-%20Prevention.pdf

Peter, T. (2009). Exploring taboos: Comparing male- and female-perpetrated child sexual abuse. *Journal of Interpersonal Violence, 24*(7), 1111–1128. doi:10.1177/0886260508322194

Pratley, J., & Goodman-Delahunty, J. (2011). Increased self-disclosure of offending by intrafamilial child sex offenders. *Sexual Abuse in Australia and New Zealand,* 3(1), 10–22.

Quadara, A., Nagy, V., Higgins, D., & Siegel, N. (2015). *Conceptualising the Prevention of Child Sexual Abuse – Final Report. Research Report.* Retrieved from https://aifs.gov.au/publications/conceptualising-prevention-child-sexual-abuse

Reid, B. (1998). *An Exploration of Tactics used by Perpetrators of Intrafamilial Child Sexual Assault.* (PhD), University of New South Wales Sydney, Australia. Retrieved from http://www.unsworks.unsw.edu.au/primo_library/libweb/action/dlDisplay.do?vid=UNSWORKS&docId=unsworks_40041

Russell, D. (1986). *The Secret Trauma: Incest in the Lives of Girls and Women.* New York: Basic Books.

Stathopoulos, M. (2014, March). The exception that proves the rule: Female sex offending and the gendered nature of sexual violence. *ACSSA Research Summary.* Retrieved from https://aifs.gov.au/publications/exception-proves-rule

Ward, T. (2002). The management of risk and the design of good lives. *Australian Psychologist,* 37(3), 172–179. doi:10.1080/00050060210001706846

Ward, T., & Beech, A. R. (2015). Dynamic risk factors: A theoretical dead-end? *Psychology, Crime and Law,* 21(2), 100–113.

Ward, T., & Fortune, C. (2016). From dynamic risk factors to causal processes: A methodological framework. *Psychology Crime & Law,* 22(1–2), 190–202.

White, M., & Epston, D. (1989). *Literate Means to Therapeutic Ends.* Adelaide: Dulwich Centre Publications.

Wijkman, M., Bijleveld, C., & Hendriks, J. (2010). Women don't do such things! Characteristics of female sex offenders and offender types. *Sexual Abuse: A Journal of Research and Treatment,* 22(2).

# Chapter 4

# Mothers

## Introduction

No family member has been more scrutinized or has attracted more opprobrium than the mother. Over more than half a century, ideas that women bear primary or equal responsibility for their partner's choice to sexually abuse a child have proved extraordinarily powerful and enduring, both in the popular mind and in professional responses. Programs that offer therapy to all members of the family carry the legacy of earlier approaches to family therapy that allocated responsibility to non-offending mothers. In contrast, the Cedar Cottage Program took a strong stand that held the harming father totally accountable for the decision to abuse a child, the tactics employed to evade responsibility and enforce secrecy and for the consequences for the victim and family.

The approach to working with women described in this chapter outlines the ways in which the accountability of the harming father is operationalized to avoid the mother-blaming that is embedded in institutional responses to incest. Understanding the operations of the core dynamics of responsibility, secrecy, protection/loyalty and resistance, outlined in Chapter 2, is central to working in non-judgemental and empowering ways with women who are mothering in the aftermath of disclosure of incest.

## The enduring theme of maternal culpability

The enduring nature of mother-blaming suggests that it is useful to place it in its historical context and to trace the ways in which certain core ideas have re-emerged over time. Early literature in psychiatry, child protection and paediatrics proposed the theory that incest was a product of *dysfunctional families*. In the era before the family as an institution came under feminist critique for its gendered power imbalances, women were seen as responsible for family well-being, and therefore for the family dysfunction that was seen to underpin incest. Measured against sexist standards for women and mothers, the deficits of these women – described in the clinical literature in pejorative terms such as

## 58 Mothers

'frigid', 'dependent' (Machotka, Pittman, & Flomenhaft, 1967, p. 100); and 'cold', 'distant', 'potentially attractive but untidy and unkempt' (Eist & Mandel, 1968, p. 218) – rendered them failures, driving their partner to sexually abuse a child. Their role in the family was characterized as 'the cornerstone in the pathological family system' (Lustig, Dresser, Spellman, & Murray, 1966, p. 39). A recurrent theme in this literature was that women are aware of and even further, *collude* with the sexual abuse of their child:

> The most striking finding concerning the wives of incestuous fathers is their knowledge of and collusion in the incestuous affair ... in almost every case the wife promoted the incestuous relationship by abandoning or frustrating their husbands sexually, or by actively altering the living arrangements to foster incest.
>
> (Sarles, 1975, p. 637)

A second theme was that it is the woman's absence, conceptualized as *abandoning* her husband that precipitates incest. This abandonment could involve gaining employment outside the home, being ill, hospitalization or attempting to leave a violent partner. In this literature, it is unquestioned that the abandoned father responds by turning to his daughter to meet his unfulfilled sexual and emotional needs. In terms of the core dynamic of responsibility, it is clear that the focus on mothers and their alleged culpability represented a gross misallocation of the responsibility of the father for his decision to sexually abuse a child.

Although these mother-blaming ideas appear shocking in the modern context, they have proved stubbornly resilient over time, albeit expressed in less pejorative terms. For example, they appeared in several influential child protection texts and treatment programs that emerged in response to the 'discovery' of child sexual assault in the late 1970s and early 1980s. A notable example is seen in Sgroi's (1982) ground-breaking text on responding to child sexual abuse, where the theme of the absent or abandoning mother appeared in the characterizations of non-offending mothers as *psychologically absent* and theme of the collusive, culpable mother is expressed through the notion of *failing to protect*. Again, core responsibility for incest is attributed to the mother:

> For whatever combination of reasons, one of the characteristics of the 'psychologically absent' mothers of incest victims is to fail to protect by failing to limit inappropriate behaviour between their husbands and children.
>
> (Sgroi, 1982, p. 193)

In early treatment programs that developed during the 1980s, a shift can be detected from placing primary responsibility with the mother, to a notion of shared parental responsibility for incest, exemplified in the naming of the Giaretto program as *Parents United*. Continuing to draw on the theory of incest as a result of family dysfunction, the aim of treatment was that each parent takes responsibility for their role in allowing incest to occur in the family. Ensuring that the mother took her share of responsibility was a key treatment goal.

> The mother may not always be aware of the sources of her guilt, but in time she usually will admit to strong wrenches of guilt for not fulfilling her role as mother and wife. If she had ministered to the needs of her family instead of her own selfish wants, the incestuous events would not have occurred, had she met her husband's emotional and sexual needs, he would not have turned to her daughter for satisfying them, had she kept her eyes and ears open, she would have caught the situation and been able to protect her daughter.
>
> (Giaretto, 1982, p.37)

Therapeutic approaches underpinned by notions of incest arising from family dysfunction emphasize the importance of the apology session (Furniss, Bingley-Miller, & Bentovim, 1984; Giaretto, 1982). As exemplified by Trepper and Barrett, this approach to the harming father's apology mutualizes responsibility between the parents:

> [T]he abusing father apologizes publicly to the entire family for the facts of the abuse, and verbally takes responsibility for it. The nonabusing mother apologizes for her part in the abuse; for example, she might apologize for not encouraging the type of relationship with her daughter that would have allowed the girl to tell her when the abuse was actually occurring.
>
> (Trepper and Barrett, 1989, p. 47)

This approach to intervention fails to account for the tactics, discussed in the previous chapter, by which the harming father sets up the conditions for the abuse, including undermining the mother–child relationship. Nor do these ideas take into account the potentially disabling effects on women of co-existing domestic violence, which is common in families where a parent sexually harms a child (Alaggia & Turton, 2005; Kellogg & Menard, 2003).

The continuing attribution of responsibility to the non-offending mother can be seen more recently in a study by Lev-Weisel (2006), where the description of the 'unwitting accomplice' mother echoes the theme of the collusive mother. A recent paper exploring differences between extra and intra-familial offenders (Seto, Babchishin, Pullman, & McPhail, 2015) reprised the theories discussed earlier about the quality of the spousal relationship as a causative factor in incest: '[T]he mother is sexually and emotionally unavailable; for example, a father may turn to his eldest daughter to fulfil his sexual and

# 60 Mothers

emotional needs because his spouse is depressed, disinterested in having sex with him, or are not getting along' (p. 54).

Ideas such as these about mothers and their responsibility for family well-being do not exist in a vacuum but are shaped by the ideology of motherhood.

> [T]he good mother is ... that formidable social construct placing pressure on women to conform to particular standards and ideals, against which they are judged and judge themselves. The good mother is also recognised as institutionalised in social arrangements and social practices, and hence operating beyond the belief systems or choices of individual women.
>
> (Goodwin & Huppatz, 2010, pp. 1–2)

The enduring and powerful nature of ideas that allocate responsibility to mothers is also seen in their prominence in popular discourse, demonstrated starkly by the ways in which they are drawn on by offenders in seeking to explain and excuse their abusive behaviour. For example, when men first entered the Cedar Cottage Program it was common for them to attribute blame for the sexual abuse to the failings of their wives.

> My wife often was depressed and wanted to kill herself. It didn't make me feel good, having a wife like that. I was lonely. (Bob)
>
> I'm very demanding sexually. I like to be loved, scratching my back, fingers running through my hair. She's not that kind. I was starved and sexually hyperactive. (Shane)

This long history of apportioning responsibility to women for their partner's decision to sexually abuse has been vigorously challenged by feminist scholars and activists, who exposed the ways in which the underlying sexist assumptions about family roles and responsibilities had unfairly promoted mother-blame while simultaneously exonerating men from accountability for their abusive behaviours and their effects on all family members (Davies & Krane, 2006; Hooper, 1992; Ward, 1984; Wattenberg, 1985).

Feminist studies using qualitative methodologies gave voice to the lived experience of women when they faced the crisis of disclosure of child sexual abuse within their family, promoting greater empathy for, and understanding of, the multiple ways in which women may respond to the crisis of disclosure (for example, Alaggia, 2001; Hooper, 1992). The resulting body of literature provided a more nuanced and complex understanding of women's responses (Alaggia, 2002; Hooper & Humphreys, 1998), which conceptualized these as fluid and changing, in contrast to earlier static and binary notions, which suggested that in the midst of the shock of disclosure, women should immediately believe, protect and support their children (Carlton & Krane, 2013).

## The crisis of disclosure

It is difficult to comprehend the magnitude of the crisis into which a woman is catapulted when she is told that her intimate partner has sexually abused her child/ren. Despite the beliefs about maternal culpability and failure in families where a father sexually abuses a child, it is worth noting that children in the Cedar Cottage Program disclosed to their mothers more frequently than to any other person (Mason, 2009). The words of women interviewed on intake into the Cedar Cottage provide some examples of the strong and mixed emotions evoked by the crisis of disclosure.

> I was in shock, traumatised. It destroyed me, like an atomic reaction. I felt sick, numb, dead. (Mary)
>
> It was a day I don't think I'll ever forget. Horrible. I didn't know how to feel, didn't know what to think, I didn't know if it was true or not true. Something was telling me it was true, something else was telling me 'no it can't be'. (Sarah)
>
> I hated him with everything. I could have done anything to him, I really despised him, I literally hated him and I hated my daughter for doing this to me. (Joy)

The child protection system's prescription for women's responses to the crisis of disclosure of sexual abuse by an intimate partner is typically that they believe the allegations immediately and choose to support the victimized child (or children) over their partner. Many factors can influence the course of this process for women, such as financial dependence on the partner, being a victim of domestic violence, the potential material and emotional losses faced and pre-existing stressors (Bolen & Krane, 2013). What is rarely addressed in the literature, but which emerged from the practice of the Cedar Cottage Program, is the role that the harming father plays in influencing the mother's response to disclosure. This can be either or both through the type of tactics deployed prior to the disclosure, or to tactics employed after the disclosure. For example, carefully cultivating a picture of the child as a liar over a long period of time provides a layer of protection for the abuser by creating a context in which the child's fear of not being believed is heightened; should the child disclose, this tactic creates barriers to the mother's believing the child. Men interviewed as they progressed through the program admitted that their tactics included planning to both prevent and to deal with possible disclosure.

> Everything I did was planned, it was all to do with planning ... even down to getting [my daughter] in a frame of mind where she couldn't tell anyone what was going on, planning and trying for it not to be disclosed. Everything was planned, I always had an excuse if she did disclose to be ready to blame someone else. (Ross)

## 62 Mothers

Tactics which the men reported using to try to minimize their accountability when the abuse was revealed included ensuring that their partner was not aware of the full extent of the sexual behaviours. They achieved this by controlling their partner's access to information, offering an immediate apology with promises of rebuilding the relationship and, most damagingly for women and children, providing a version of the events that painted the child as culpable:

> He said it was all her fault, she wouldn't leave him alone. (Louise)
>
> Yes, my daughter initiated it. He told me she'd call him into the bedroom. (Paula)

These examples highlight the importance of the therapist attempting to understand the interactional context of the woman and her partner, empathically exploring her reactions and thoughts as she grapples with mixed feelings, shock and uncertainty, rather than cutting off communication about these painful issues by simply demanding that she focus solely on believing and supporting the child.

Women who do not follow the prescription of immediate belief and support are judged to have 'failed to protect' and risk having their child/ren removed from their care by child protection services. Krane, Strega and Carlton (2013) argue that embedding this concept in child protection legislation, policy and practice in many Western nations reveals that: '[T]hese policies and practices reflect longstanding and deeply embedded mother-blaming and father-absenting ideologies that shape Anglo-American child protection systems' (p. 23).

This prescription for mothers fails to take account of important research which deconstructs concepts such as *ambivalence, belief* and *support*, which are commonly used but poorly operationalized in child protection investigations of non-offending mothers. Bolen and Krane (2013) argue that maternal ambivalence and support can coexist.

> [A] mother can certainly be ambivalent about her child's disclosure of sexual abuse and about what to do about it but this ambivalence does not therefore mean that the mother cannot or will not be supportive of her child post-disclosure.
>
> (pp. 81–82)

Similarly, coming to a position of believing that the sexual abuse has occurred is a complex process, rather than a one-off event, which cannot be simply understood as belief or disbelief. Again, this may or may not be related to the support which a woman is able to provide to her child.

However, in the pressured and fast-paced context of child protection intervention, where decisions focus of necessity on immediate child safety, the complexity of considerations such as these is easily overlooked. Given the enduring ideas about maternal culpability and collusion in intra-familial child sexual abuse, it is likely that many women experience the initial interventions by police and child protection services around disclosure and investigation as judgemental, negative and lacking empathy. On entering the Cedar Cottage Program, Julie described her experience in this way: 'CPS acted like I knew. They said: "What sort of a mother are you?"'

The nature of these initial encounters will influence women's perception of the service system, and can present challenges for their engagement in the therapeutic process; challenges which can provide the harming father with the opportunity to align himself with his partner, isolating her from support and interfering with efforts to engage her. Women can also be isolated through shame and guilt that lead them to conceal the cause of their separation from friends and extended family. For example, on entering the program, Suzie, who had moved to escape the shame of neighbours knowing about the abuse, talked of her partner in these terms: 'He is my only support'. A woman's isolation provides the harming father with the opportunity to continue to try to exert control over her perception of events and in particular, the issue of responsibility. This speaks to the power of engaging the woman in group work with others who have faced the same assault on their family life and betrayal by their intimate partner. Where this is not possible, facilitating contact between the woman and another who has been through the same crisis can be a powerful antidote to secrecy, shame and isolation.

## Therapeutic work with mothers

### Engagement and initial phase

Given the preceding discussion about the crisis of disclosure, the pervasive mother-blaming culture of many investigative services and the offender's interest in maintaining his partner's isolation, it is understandable that many women will be apprehensive about therapeutic engagement. The strength of the prevailing discourse of maternal responsibility for incest will have many women blaming themselves, as well as experiencing blame and judgement from others, for the harm that their child has suffered. Others may be angry at their referral, for example if they believe that the family can sort out the issues on their own, or if they believe that offering treatment to the offender is too lenient a response and a solely criminal justice response is more appropriate.

In the light of understandably strong emotions, it is important for therapists to explore with the woman her experience and reactions to the crisis engendered by finding out about the sexual abuse, including her interactions with services, the harming father and the victim/s. What does she know, what does she not know, and what are the sources of her information? Most importantly, in a program in which the harming father is concurrently in therapy, what would she like to find out?

A non-judgemental, strengths-based approach is required to counter the self-blame and shame that women commonly experience. A core aspect of shame is the woman's emotional attachment to her partner. Sheinberg and Fraenkel (2001) argue that it is essential to enable discussion of, and to validate, the woman's bond with her partner rather than to have this unspoken and unacknowledged. Building a relationship, in which the woman is able to discuss difficult issues such as this, anger at the child victim and doubts about the allegations, is essential.

Findings from research by Bolen, Dessel and Sutter (2015) on the multi-dimensional nature of the support that non-offending carers provide to children can inform practice with mothers. This research highlighted the complexity encompassed within the term *support* and identified eight dimensions of support: basic needs, safety and protection, decision-making, active parenting, instrumental support, availability, sensitivity to the child, and affirmation. This provides a wide canvass for strengths-based discussions about the ways in which the mother is responding to the child, as opposed to narrow, binary discussions about *belief* and *support*.

As described previously, disclosure evokes a range of tactics from the harming father, aimed at deflecting his responsibility for the abuse, including onto the child, his partner or factors such as work stress or alcohol. Central to these tactics is his attempt to limit the information available to his partner. For example, he may discourage her from reading the child's statement, or work hard to establish a version of the abuse that reduces his responsibility. If he can establish himself as the main source of information, his power to control the situation is enhanced.

> I did after about a week get to see the first page of her statement, and that was it, the rest, everything else I know, is what [my partner] has told me. (Sarah)
> I don't know what my daughter has said against her father. I've seen no statements, and we've never discussed it. (Lorraine)

The harming father may also continue a pattern in their relationship where his needs are central and his partner is encouraged to put him first, above her interests and those of other family members, including the victimized child. For example, he may work hard at enlisting her help for whatever he portrays as the reason for the abuse and imply that she holds some of the blame. Through intensive interactions with her – apologising, wooing, and promising a better relationship – the harming father seeks to ensure that his needs come first.

> [Him] not wanting me to go to work of a night, he'd say 'just ring in sick and not go'. I think now he was asking for help but he had no one there

to help him. Because it never happened when I was home. It was only when I went to work two nights a week type of thing. (Maria)

Where his tactics used to set up and hide the sexual abuse have undermined the mother–child relationship, the harming father may seek to continue to keep them apart, for example by taking on the role of the mother's supporter in her efforts to deal with a child who may be angry, silent and difficult, while continuing to promote division between them.

My husband and daughter have never got on, now what has happened has given her a lot of power – more 'ammunition'. She is angry with me all the time. To a degree she has been like this for two or three years but now she's ten times worse, no a hundred times. Now I can't control her at all. (Rosa)

As described in the previous chapter, these types of tactics aimed at limiting the information available to the mother and centralizing the man's needs are at odds with the program's requirement that the man take personal responsibility for his behaviour. If he does take up the treatment program's invitation to take a stand of personal responsibility, the initial crisis of discovery for the woman is followed by further crises as his revelations about the range of tactics used to establish and hide the abuse reveal the depth of the betrayal by her partner. This can also include naming many of her experiences as intimate partner violence, particularly when this coercive, controlling violence has taken forms other than physical abuse. Strong, non-judgemental engagement with the mother can provide her with support as she enters the subsequent stages of therapy, where she has access to information that can provide her with new perspectives on the tactics to which she, the victim and other family members have been subjected.

This discussion of the impact of the man's ongoing tactics on non-offending mothers does not mean that the woman is understood as a passive victim lacking agency. Women in this situation are required to respond to the emotional and material needs of their children; to cope with the intrusion into the family's life of services with the power to remove children; and to deal with their own shock, distress and confusion. Validation by the therapist of the ways that the woman has responded to these demands is important and comes from a position of acknowledging that the woman is making decisions in the best interests of herself and her family as she sees them. With different information, new possibilities are open to her, but the path is painful and challenging.

### Unravelling tactics and re-evaluating important relationships

As the offender faces up to the extent of the abuse and details the tactics by which he set up the conditions for abuse and maintained secrecy, including after disclosure, women are confronted with extremely painful information about the layers of deception and betrayal to which they and the child have been subjected.

> It gets more and more as it goes on. When you think there's nothing left, it hits you like a ton of bricks that there's more left! (Sarah)

Therapy now enters a new stage where the woman is provided with information that challenges her previous understandings about her relationship with her partner and with the victimized child. In contrast to the picture that the harming father attempted to paint of himself as caring and reformed following disclosure, women receive new information that enables them to see him in a different light, as self-centred.

> He was very uncaring and just didn't seem to, didn't even care about consequences – how it would affect me, how would it affect my daughter, never entered his mind. (Lorraine)
>
> Well, I think his idea was that he was the end all and be all, he had the final say in whatever ... I don't know, just the whole, just putting himself first and everybody else last. (Liz)

For many women, learning about the tactics of entrapment to which the child was subjected, and the ways in which they were deceived, begins to provide answers to the many questions with which they are grappling – even if unspoken – such as why their child kept the secret about the abuse and about how they were not aware of what was happening in their home.

> You go through wondering if the child liked it, it goes through a mother's mind, well why did they leave it for so long, they must have wanted to do it, they must have, things like that. (Louise)
>
> Now I think of it is, when I used to go to bed early, he'd come up, quite often I'd just go to bed and read, he'd keep coming up, it never worried me, I just thought he was coming up over concern. He was coming up to check if I was asleep, you know! (Julie)
>
> He kept saying: 'Don't tell mum it will destroy her' constantly saying that all the time. (Liz)

Hearing from the partner about his deliberate tactics of deceit and secrecy can relieve the woman's guilt and self-blame about not having been able to prevent the abuse of the child.

> But in the beginning you do blame yourself. You feel guilty, but you know as it goes on that there's no way you could have known, because of the way it was done. (Joy)

If their partner faces up about the ways in which he entrapped the child, the women are provided with information which enables them to see what happened through the eyes of the child. This is a very different experience to their partner's previous efforts to keep his needs and perspective central. This information can provide a foundation for the woman and child to begin rebuilding their relationship, which has been harmed by the harming father's efforts to divide them, their division being essential to keeping the abuse secret.

> The way he was so cunning, the way he made it hard for her to disclose. I find that very difficult, I didn't think he could do anything like that. The things he said to her – 'If you tell anybody you'll break up the family' things like that. He made it so hard for her, made her feel guilty, blaming her for what was happening. (Lydia)

In the excerpt below, Joy explains how a session in which her partner faced up to a tactic that had driven a wedge between herself and her daughter provided her with new information and new hope for building a better relationship with her daughter.

> I couldn't get any respect from her. She wouldn't do anything that I said. He had told her that the abuse was my fault, every time, not every time he abused her, say five times out of ten, he had said to her: 'I'm doing this, it's your mother's fault'. You couldn't expect a child to have much respect for a mother. I didn't know he had said that. That was news to me, and made it a little bit easier, I could talk to her about it, and also he did tell me that by doing this he had made her feel like an outcast in the family, even though he had gone from home.

Detailed discussion of the issues involved in conducting conjoint sessions between family members, including sessions in which the harming father 'faces up' to his partner, is provided in Chapter 7. Joy's story provides an example of the ways in which the offender facing up can provide new information that broadens the scope for women's responses. Therapy offers a safe context in which the woman can explore her reactions to the unravelling of the harming father's tactics and their effects on the victim, on the mother–victim relationship and on other family relationships. Group work, as discussed in Chapter 11, provides a context in which women can share their experiences with others who are going through similar painful experiences.

As the tactics are revealed, the woman also re-evaluates her relationship with her partner, which brings accompanying feelings of anger, grief and betrayal.

> Actually before it would have been, how they say 'love is blind', and you go blind for everything, but not now, that doesn't get in the way anymore. They open up your eyes a lot, in how the bloke manipulates everybody and

how you kind of think you've got a perfect marriage, and when you really think about it, it wasn't that perfect as you thought it was. (Lily)

If treatment discourages the harming father from his initial responses of continuing to centralize his needs above others, and exposes his controlling behaviours, the women are in a stronger position from which to make decisions about the future of their relationship with their partner.

But the men want a surety. How can you give them a surety? Some of the women when they go in there, the men expect them to stand by them, whatever, so they can face up. But if they're doing that, they're still controlling their wives. (June)

One challenging but often unspoken part of the woman's re-evaluation of the relationship with her partner is her decision-making about resuming a sexual relationship with him and her reactions when and if she does so. This is an element of the relationship that may be so infused with shame that women are unlikely to raise it in therapy. Hence, the therapist needs to initiate discussion in a way that opens safe space for discussion of this topic. It is likely that women will have many painful questions, such as: When he was with me sexually, was he thinking about my daughter? When he was with my daughter, was he thinking about me? Through discussion in therapy the woman can express her pain at the betrayal of the relationship by her partner and can be supported to formulate questions which she needs her partner to answer as part of his facing up. If the therapist does not broach this taboo topic, the harming father will be the only person talking about this with her, leaving him with scope to avoid facing up to this core betrayal of her trust.

The women's comments in this chapter provide examples of the powerful impacts of the harming father taking responsibility for his actions, by explicitly making transparent the complex web of behaviours through which he abused the child and attempted to disable the mother as a potential resource to assist the child. However, not all harming fathers take up the invitation to accept responsibility. In similar ways to those by which they divided mother and children to enable their abuse, some men employed tactics of division between the Cedar Cottage Program and their partners. In order to remain in the program, they may make some limited disclosures, but may try to avoid fully facing up to their partners. This can result in continuing division between the women and the victims. For example, Margaret described how her partner Steve continued to assert to her the victim's complicity in the abuse, all the while appearing to be facing up in his therapy at the program.

He always denied that part, he always said that she never ever said 'no' and like I said to Steve, 'you can't blame her, she's sitting there at the police station, she's so confused, of course she's going to say to them well I said no but dad made me', because they don't know what the police are going to think or do. He never held that against her, he never called her a liar, he just said to me that she never said no. He agreed to her police statement (at the program), but to me that's the only part he didn't agree with, he said 'I want you to know all the rest is true'. But he said she never said no at any time, that's what he wanted me to know.

In this example, Steve is presenting himself as honest (in contrast to his step-daughter) and empathic about her encounter with the police, all the while attempting to erect a barrier to the potential for Margaret and her daughter to be able to discuss the coercion that she experienced. He continued to undermine the mother–daughter relationship while appearing to be concerned and honest.

## Conclusion

Therapy with the mother involves supporting her through the painful process of unravelling the effects of the harming father's tactics on herself, her relationship with her partner, and with the victimized child and other family members. These tactics have promoted secrecy and divided family members, and have required family members to place loyalty to the harming father's interests and needs above those of other family members. It is important that these tactics are placed in the context of their key purpose – to overcome the resistance of the victim child and to undermine the mother's potential as her ally. Equally, the victim's and the mother's resistance to these tactics, both before and after disclosure are explored and validated. The ways in which children resist in the face of oppressive abuse is discussed further in the following chapter.

## References

Alaggia, R. (2001). Cultural and religious influences in maternal response to intrafamilial child sexual abuse: Charting new territory for research and treatment. *Journal of Child Sexual Abuse, 10*(2), 41–60. doi:10.1300/J070v10n02_03

Alaggia, R. (2002). Balancing acts: Reconceptualizing support in maternal response to intra-familial child sexual abuse. *Clinical Social Work Journal, 30*(1), 41–56. doi:10.1023/a:1014274311428

Alaggia, R., & Turton, J. V. (2005). Against the odds: The impact of woman abuse on maternal response to disclosure of child sexual abuse. *Journal of Child Sexual Abuse, 14*(4), 95–113. doi:10.1300/J070v14n04_05

Bolen, R. M., Dessel, A. B., & Sutter, J. (2015). Parents will be parents: Conceptualizing and measuring nonoffending parent and other caregiver support following disclosure of sexual abuse. *Journal of Aggression Maltreatment & Trauma, 24*(1), 41–67. doi:10.1080/10926771.2015.1005267

## 70 Mothers

Bolen, R. M., & Krane, J. (2013). What do we really know about maternal failure to protect in cases of child sexual abuse? In S. Strega, J. Krane, S. Lapierre, C. Richardson, & R. Carlton (Eds.), *Failure to Protect: Moving Beyond Gendered Responses* (pp. 77–91). Winnipeg, Manitoba: Fernwood Publishing.

Carlton, R., & Krane, J. (2013). Neither shaken nor stirred: The persistence of maternal failure to protect in cases of child sexual abuse. In S. Strega, J. Krane, S. Lapierre, C. Richardson, & R. Carlton (Eds.), *Failure to Protect: Moving Beyond Gendered Responses* (pp. 30–48). Winnipeg, Manitoba: Fernwood Publishing.

Davies, L., & Krane, J. (2006). Collaborate with caution: protecting children, helping mothers. *Critical Social Policy*, 26(2), 412–425.

Eist, H. I., & Mandel, A. U. (1968). Family treatment of ongoing incest behavior. *Family Process*, 7(2), 216–232. doi:10.1111/j.1545-5300.1968.00216.x

Furniss, T., Bingley-Miller, L., & Bentovim, A. (1984). Therapeutic approach to sexual abuse. *Archives of Disease in Childhood*, 59(9), 865–870.

Giaretto, H. (1982). *Integrated Treatment of Child Sexual Abuse*. Palo Alto: Science and Behaviour Books, Inc.

Goodwin, S., & Huppatz, K. (2010). The good mother in theory and research: an overview. In S. Goodwin & K. Huppatz (Eds.), *The Good Mother: Contemporary Motherhoods in Australia* (pp. 1–24). Sydney: Sydney University Press.

Hooper, C. A. (1992). *Mothers Surviving Child Sexual Abuse*. London: Tavistock/Routledge.

Hooper, C. A., & Humphreys, C. (1998). Women whose children have been sexually abused: Reflections on a debate. *British Journal of Social Work*, 28(4), 565–580.

Kellogg, N. D., & Menard, S. W. (2003). Violence among family members of children and adolescents evaluated for sexual abuse. *Child Abuse & Neglect*, 27(12), 1367–1376.

Krane, J., Strega, S., & Carlton, R. (2013). G-d couldn't be everywhere so he created mothers: The impossibe mandate of maternal protection in child welfare. In S. Strega, J. Krane, S. Lapierre, C. Richardson, & R. Carlton (Eds.), *Failure to Protect: Moving Beyond Gendered Responses* (pp. 11–29). Winnipeg, Manitoba: Fernwood Publishing.

Lev-Weisel, R. (2006). Intergenerational transmission of sexual abuse? Motherhood in the shadow of incest. *Journal of Child Sexual Abuse, 15*(2), 75–101. doi:10.1300/J070v15n02_06

Lustig, C., Dresser, C. W., Spellman, M. W., & Murray, M. B. (1966). Incest: A family group survival pattern. *Archives of General Psychiatry, 14*(1), 31–40. doi:10.1001/archpsyc.1966.01730070033004

Machotka, P., Pittman, F. S., & Flomenhaft, K. (1967). Incest as a family affair. *Family Process, 6*(1), 98–116. doi:10.1111/j.1545-5300.1967.00098.x

Mason, A. (2009). *Factors Influencing Disclosure and Reporting of Intrafamilial Child Sexual Abuse*. Unpublished Masters thesis, University of New South Wales.

Sarles, R. (1975). Incest. *Pediatric Clinics of North America*, 22, 633–642.

Seto, M. C., Babchishin, K. M., Pullman, L. E., & McPhail, I. V. (2015). The puzzle of intrafamilial child sexual abuse: A meta-analysis comparing intrafamilial and extrafamilial offenders with child victims. *Clinical Psychology Review, 39*, 42–57. doi:10.1016/j.cpr.2015.04.001

Sgroi, S. M. (Ed.) (1982). *Handbook of Clinical Intervention in Child Sexual Abuse*. Massachusetts: Lexington Books.

Sheinberg, M., & Fraenkel, P. (2001). *The Relational Trauma of Incest: A Family Based Approach to Treatment*. New York: The Guilford Press

Trepper, T. S., & Barrett, M. J. (1989). *Systemic Treatment of Incest*. New York: Brunner/Mazel.

Ward, E. (1984). *Father Daughter Rape*. London: The Women's Press Ltd.

Wattenberg, E. (1985). In a different light: A feminist perspective on the role of mothers in father-daughter incest. *Child Welfare*, 64(3), 203–211.

Chapter 5

# Children who have experienced parental sexual assault

## Introduction

The child victim of parental sexual abuse experiences a profound violation of trust and is faced with an insoluble dilemma – a parent on whom she relies for love, nurturance and safety, is also harming her. In addition to this violation of her bodily integrity, autonomy and trust, the child suffers the consequences of the harming father's tactics, which are calculated to overcome her resistance and to entrap her into maintaining secrecy about the abuse. Because these consequences include the disruption of her relationships with all family members, treatment that includes all family members (though not traditional conjoint family therapy) holds the potential to rebuild the victim child's relationship with her mother and siblings. Information from her father's therapy may also be useful in her recovery and some children may value some form of restitution or acknowledgement of his responsibility. In decisions about important aspects of therapy such as this, safety and restoring the child's sense of autonomy are central considerations. In this approach, all therapists working with the family and particularly those working with the harming father need to be vigilant about avoiding replicating the patterns of intrusion and responsibility-shifting that characterized the harming father's abusive behaviour.

## Experiences of the harming father's tactics and their impact

Because of his intimate knowledge about the child, the harming father is able to carefully tailor the tactics of entrapment both to the child's developmental level and to areas of vulnerability. Since the family context provides the harming father with ongoing access to his victims, these tactics are often revised and titrated over time to meet the child's growing resistance. For example, appeals to a young child to protect her father from going to jail might be replaced by physical violence or restrictions on activities with peers when the child is adolescent and threatens to tell (Christiansen & Blake, 1990). Several key themes run through the common tactics. The harming father demands that his victim prioritizes protecting him and the family; he shifts responsibility onto her in many ways; and he divides his victim from others in the family through the imposition of secrecy. In this section, examples are provided and the consequences for the child are discussed.

Appealing to the child to protect the harming father and the family places the child in an invidious position where she is pressured to sacrifice her well-being to save the family. For example, if the child's mother has struggled with mental health issues, the harming father may stress the impact of any disclosure on the mother's health and ability to care for the child and other children. Some children endure the abuse in an effort to protect siblings from suffering the same fate. In the extract below, Sarah, 16 years old, talks about the burden of the protective role from her perspective, looking back at the end of therapy.

> You don't care about yourself, you don't like to get close to anyone and you feel very lonely. You have no self-worth, you don't care about yourself and you know, you think what happens to you doesn't matter, you're just more worried about everyone else and protecting everyone else.

Also evident in Sarah's words is the isolation that children experience as a consequence of the harming father's actions aimed at disrupting relationships with family members who may believe and support them if they tell. The mother–child relationship is the most common target of these tactics of division. Sometimes a harming father targets a child where there are existing difficulties in the mother–child relationship.

> There was a problem with my wife and step-daughter when I first lived with them and I never, ever tried to do anything about that, and then naturally enough when I was abusing her, I was driving an even bigger wedge between them. (Bob)

When a step-father exploits a pre-existing troubled mother–child relationship in order to isolate and abuse the child, he creates a context in which the child is unlikely to disclose to her mother. If his abuse is exposed, the likelihood of the mother believing and supporting the child in the face of his denials is reduced. For example, Margaret had escaped a violent relationship with her daughter's father and found a new and much happier relationship with David. Her daughter Stephanie had presented a range of behavioural problems since the separation of her parents and had always been antagonistic to David's joining the family. After Stephanie's disclosure to a school teacher, Margaret responded angrily:

> She told because she wanted her own way. Maybe to hurt Dave and myself. She wants me to get back with her biological father. I've never had

## 74 Victimized children

real love from her like it should be. She blamed me for the separation from her father.

Another approach to undermining the mother–child relationship was described by Luigi, as he faced up to the tactics he had deployed through the process of participating in therapy at Cedar Cottage:

> I affected their relationship because I was turning my daughter against her mother in subtle ways by saying things about my wife, like my wife was stupid or didn't know what she was talking about, just things like that. Also I would have affected the way my wife would have looked at my daughter because I was promoting this image to my wife that our daughter was always the one that was at fault, she was the one that was always causing the trouble.

The effects of the harming father's tactics commonly compound and multiply over time. For example, under pressure to remain silent to protect their families, victims can find that their protective silence creates further barriers between themselves and their mothers at the point of disclosure when their need for belief and support is at its highest.

> My mum just couldn't understand what had gone on and whose fault it really was and things like that. She didn't blame me directly, she didn't blame me, but she sort of implied that I had something to do with it you know, because I hadn't told earlier. (Amelia)

The distance between children and their mothers means that the victims can be left with perceptions about their mother's role in the abuse, with no avenue available to check out the veracity of these perceptions. One of the most harmful of these is the belief that the mother knew about and even condoned the abuse. Sometimes this is due to the child's developmental level, where they expect that their parent will be aware of what is occurring.

> Back then I thought she knew what was happening. I thought she just knew by the way I was acting… (Lucy)
> Like I just thought she wasn't a caring mother, she could have seen what he was doing, and therefore I couldn't talk to her, I couldn't face her with it. (Megan)

In other situations, the harming father actively promotes the idea of maternal complicity. For example, Julie was shocked to realise the impression given to her daughter by the timing of the abuse by her partner.

> He said all along, 'I always made sure you were in the house', whether he said that innocently or whatever, thinking, thinking, thinking, why the hell would he say something like that? And then sort of I think, gee, my daughter must have been under the impression if I was always there, and then I checked with her and said: 'Did you think I knew because I was always there?' and she said: 'Yes'.

Therapy can unravel harmful perceptions such as these through the provision of important new information to mothers and children about the harming father's tactics of entrapment, division and concealment. The pain of the young person, who believes that her mother condoned the abuse and participated in the betrayal of trust, is incalculable. In the case of Julie and her daughter, this particular tactic was revealed through the harming father's participation in therapy and was able to inform the mother–daughter therapy. Notably the harming father did not face up to the impact of always abusing the child when the mother was in the house, leaving it to the mother to explore the implications with her daughter. Working with mothers and children together and rebuilding the mother–child relationship is discussed in more detail in chapter 7.

In addition to undermining the mother–child relationship, the harming father can further isolate the child by implementing tactics of division between the victim and their siblings. In a blended family, Joe described how he did this:

> I purposely set up a favouritism barrier between my kids and her, so that she wouldn't have any reason to think that if she told them, that they'd believe her rather than me.

One very damaging way of shifting his responsibility for the abuse involves the harming father encouraging the child's belief that they are complicit in the sexual activity. This promotes shame and guilt which are strong barriers to disclosure. Many abusers begin their abuse by seemingly 'accidental' touching of children, which is confusing. This creates a context of uncertainty, which makes it unlikely that the child will be able to resist openly as it is only after the abuse has become increasingly intrusive that children are able to definitely recognize it as such (Alaggia, Collin-Vézina, & Lateef, 2017; Berliner & Conte, 1990). As a result, the child is trapped because of the implied complicity of not having actively resisted at the start. In her study of father–daughter incest, Phelan (1995) found that when the abuse is committed by a parent in the child's home, there are multiple opportunities for the harming father to subtly initiate sexual abuse under the cover of routine family activities, such as checking the child's bed covers, playful wrestling and backrubs while watching television. This context of normalized family activities made it difficult for the children to identify whether the initial sexual touching was accidental. The resulting confusion and disbelief made the children hesitant to react. The power differential between the parent and child is reflected in the finding that any

## 76 Victimized children

negative reaction on the part of the child resulted in the parent pulling back, but only until they found another opportunity to again initiate sexual abuse. An extra-familial offender, in contrast, may desist if the child resists overtly as he does not have access to the same degree of power and authority as a parent over the child.

The entrapment of children by the blurring of the initial boundary violations with everyday family activities in itself promotes victims' perceptions of complicity. However, as they progressed in therapy, some men in the Cedar Cottage Program described how they further promoted the child's view of their complicity, for example, by talking to the child in ways which mutualized responsibility.

> And I'd draw her into it with saying: 'If I ever try to do it again, just say no' and this sort of thing, so you're making her part of it, it's her responsibility now, it's not for me to stop it, it's for her to stop me. (John)
> I had a talk to my daughter when we were sitting in the car and I told her *we're* going to stop and that's it. (Mal)

For some men, subtlety of the types of tactics described above is eschewed in favour of the imposition of a regime of violence and control over all members of the family. For the child who is being physically abused, and/or has witnessed assaults on her mother and other family members, the message that resistance will be met with further violence can be strongly made through the parent's use of violence alone.

> Yes, he hit me with the belt for doing absolutely nothing, and he used to get angry at me for doing like the littlest things, like once I dropped a plate and he hit me, and then there was one time in the car, we were at a res-taurant, this is a big one, I can remember, and I think I must have said something, it probably got him really mad, like it was offensive to him, and then he just hit me when I got home, like I wouldn't even get out of the car and he dragged me out of the car. (Jess)

Through the types of tactics described in this chapter, the harming father attempts to entrap the child in a web of secrecy, reinforced by their isolation and estrangement from other family members. The approach to therapy described in this book provides opportunities to work with all family members in ways that provide them with new information from which they can re-evaluate and rebuild fractured relationships between all those victimized by the harming father's tactics – mothers, victims and siblings.

## Disclosure/discovery

It is difficult to comprehend the courage that is required for the victim to take the risk of telling. Among many things she is risking her disclosure being met with disbelief, loss of her family, being blamed for destroying the family, and possibly violent retaliation by the harming father against herself or others about whom she cares. Some of the young women in the Cedar Cottage Program described the barriers to disclosure that their fathers had set up.

> I was worried that I'd be kicked out of home, called a liar because that used to be one of Dad's things to make out like I was a liar all the time, so I thought that if I told anyone, everyone always just calls me a liar that they would think I was lying. (Lucy)
> I didn't want to hurt mum. (Lizzie)

In the face of the harming father's carefully constructed web of isolation and entrapment, it is not surprising that many victims do not tell anyone about the abuse until adulthood (London, Bruck, Ceci, & Shuman, 2005), if at all. Research on disclosure consistently finds that victims of intra-familial abuse take longer to disclose than do victims of extra-familial abuse (Dupont, Messerschmitt, Vila, Bohu, & Rey-Salmon, 2014; Goodman-Brown, Edelstein, Goodman, Jones, & Gordon, 2003; Leach, Powell, Sharman, & Anglim, 2017).

While telling someone about the sexual abuse is the most obvious sign of victims' resistance to the harming father's efforts to entrap and silence them, it is important to remember that victims do not respond to the abuse and the accompanying tactics with passivity. For example, children describe avoiding times alone with the harming father through a variety of ruses that thwart his efforts to create opportunities to abuse. As they get older they may spend more time with friends as a way of avoiding him. Young people in the Cedar Cottage Program have reported pretending to have their period, wearing extra layers of clothing and hiding their face during the abuse to keep a part of themselves separate and also beyond his control. Because of the threat posed by the harming father and the consequences for the family, their resistance typically has to be subtle and indirect (Wade, 1997). This can work against the credibility of their disclosures since the common perception in the community is that people will respond to sexual victimization by immediately calling for assistance (Summit, 1983).

Motivations in disclosing are varied. For some it is developmental, as adolescents develop greater independence from the family; other young people have described the build-up of psychological distress creating a 'pressure cooker effect' (McElvaney & Culhane, 2017, p. 108); while for others the motivation in telling is to protect siblings from being victimized. In some situations, the abuse is discovered rather than disclosed, for example when the abuse is witnessed by someone in the family.

Based on research with preadolescent and adolescent girls, Staller and Nelson-Gardell (2005) have proposed a useful model for understanding the process of disclosure. They identified three phases. The first, is a pre-disclosure

## 78 Victimized children

stage, during which the child needs to become comfortable with naming what occurred as abuse, including re-assessing self-blame which may have accompanied her earlier, subtle entrapment and sorting through her feelings about the abuser. The importance of this process can be seen in the confusing context of intra-familial abuse, where 'normal' family life exists in parallel to secret experiences of abuse. The second phase involves the selection of a person, time and place to tell about the abuse and to deal with that person's response to the disclosure. The third phase involves the child's decisions about their on-going strategies of disclosure, including affirming or recanting their accounts of abuse. This model illustrates the complexity of disclosure, the difficult decisions with which children and young people must grapple, and the critical importance of the reactions of adults and others close to the child. This speaks to the importance of concurrent work with the non-offending parent and siblings, in order to build a supportive response for the disclosing child.

By whatever means the sexual abuse becomes known, a crisis is precipitated for the family. As discussed in Chapter 3, the default response of most abusers is denial and efforts to discredit the victim. Indeed, as part of the therapeutic process at Cedar Cottage, the men acknowledged that their planning for the abuse included a plan to thwart attempted disclosures and to undermine the child's credibility if she did disclose.

> She did attempt on three different occasions to disclose before. One was not long after I initially sexually assaulted her. She wanted to speak to her biological father about it, and I made a very elaborate move to prevent her from doing so. She was going down to see her biological father, and I told her mother that she'd been watching too much television about sexual assault, and I actually set about totally destroying any credibility my step-daughter had in the family's eyes in that regard. (Bob)

If the abuse is disclosed within the family, it may not be reported to police and child protection services. Faced with responses that confirm her worst fears, the victim may retract the allegation, or the harming father may minimize any sexual contact and promise to seek counselling. The impacts of disclosure on the non-offending mother and the dilemmas it raises for her are discussed in Chapter 4 and the perspectives of siblings at this crisis point are discussed in Chapter 6.

As disclosure is a process, rather than a one-off event, victims are likely to 'test the waters' in what they tell about the abuse and will be sensitive to the response received (Alaggia et al., 2017). For this reason, it is likely that the initial disclosure by the child will represent only small aspects of the abuse experienced. Disclosing initially to a peer can support the child on the path to disclosure, and any disclosure outside of the family raises the likelihood of involvement by statutory authorities.

However the abuse comes to light, the needs of the victims include being believed and being protected from retaliation from the offender including from being ejected from their family. For this reason, most jurisdictions in Australia and similar nations mandate reporting of child sexual abuse to child protection authorities and, as the behaviour is criminal, involvement of the police. In many jurisdictions, a joint police and child protection investigation is undertaken, combining the collection of evidence for a criminal prosecution with assessment of the child's safety (Goetzold, 2017). Participating in an investigative interview is a difficult experience for the child or young person and should be conducted by skilled professionals with good understanding of child development and of the layers of silencing and entrapment that the child needs to overcome in order to give an account of their experiences.

It is preferable that the abuser rather than the victimized child leave the home to address the risks of retaliation or pressure to recant the allegations. In cases at Cedar Cottage where the child had been ejected from, or fled the family home in the aftermath of the disclosure before the referral to the program, engagement of the young person in therapy was more difficult, and in some cases, unsuccessful. For example, one young woman went to live with her biological father who actively discouraged her participation in the program. In the victim's absence, and in the context in which her behaviour can understandably be challenging, the harming father will be quick to fill the vacuum by presenting himself to his partner in the most favourable light possible. As discussed in Chapter 4, providing the child's mother with non-judgemental support at this point of crisis is essential if she is to be in a position to offer the child support, even if she is engaged in the complex struggle around believing that her partner is capable of sexually abusing her child.

## Relieving protection, secrecy and responsibility and acknowledging resistance

The first part of this chapter described the complex ways in which the harming father entraps and seeks to silence the victim. The approach to therapy described in this book aims to work in ways that disentangle the victim from this web of entrapment and rebuild her relationships with her mother and siblings. Narrative approaches are useful in facilitating this process as they enable the therapist to ask questions that can enable the young person to overcome shame and self-blame that are typically legacies of the harming father's tactics. Simple assurances that children are not responsible for the abuse and for the family crisis that follows disclosure are rarely sufficient to lift the burden of guilt that the harming father's tactics have coached in the child, often over protracted periods of time. Narrative approaches, in contrast, ask questions about the harming father's behaviours that can provide new information for the young person in making sense of their experiences (Laing & Kamsler, 1990).

## 80 Victimized children

Central to this approach is the externalizing of presenting problems (White, 2007; White & Epston, 1989). Externalizing is an approach that locates problems outside the person, so that the person (and their supporters) can join together to tackle the problem. In this way, it avoids seeing problems as totalizing of the person. For example, guilt and shame may be talked about as 'self-blame'; pressure to protect the family as 'super-responsibility'; and tactics of abuse can be talked about as 'trickery'. The effects of the abuse, such as fear, can also be externalized. For example, the therapist may ask questions such as:

> How did your dad encourage self-blame to become so strong in your life?
> What has self-blame had you thinking about yourself? What has it had you doing?
> What types of things did your dad say that encouraged your habit of super-responsibility for caring for everyone in your family?
> How did he encourage fear to grow so big in your life? How has fear got in the way of you doing the things that you would like to do?

These types of questions place accountability for the sexual abuse on the harming father and encourage the young person to reflect in new ways on their experiences of their interactions with him. While lifting misplaced responsibility from the victimized child, these questions also provoke the child's reassessment of their relationship more broadly with the harming father. This can open new levels of pain for the child as the depth of his betrayal is revealed. For example, where the development of a 'special' relationship was used as a tactic to facilitate the sexual abuse, the child gains a new understanding of this relationship, which brings a profound sense of loss and betrayal.

Similar types of questions can also be asked about the impact of the harming father's tactics on the young person's relationships with her mother and other family members. For example:

> How did your dad encourage you to maintain secrecy about what he was doing?
> How did secrecy get in the way of you reaching out to others in your family for help?
> How did he encourage doubt that your mum would believe you if you told?
> How did he cause trouble between you and your brothers and sisters?

In response, young people can identify the tactics that have been used to divide them from other family members. For example, Jackie reflected on how her dad had appeared to back her up when she was in trouble with her mum, not out of concern, but for his own ends:

> He used to let me get away with a lot. I'd come home from school and mum would go through my books and say, 'Look she hadn't done this and

this', and he'd come in and say, 'Just leave her alone, just let her do it at her own pace' ... all to keep me quiet.

These types of questions map the effects of the harming father's behaviours in the young person's life and on their relationships. Core to narrative and similarly to response-based approaches is the assumption that oppression is never total and that victims always resist efforts to abuse and overwhelm them. Thus it is also important to ask questions that put the young person in touch with the ways in which they exercised agency and resisted the abuse.

> Despite your dad's pressure to give in to secrecy, how were you able to get the courage to tell?
> Despite your dad's encouragement of self-blame, how were you able to say to yourself that what he was doing was not right?
> What did it take to stand up to fear and take a stand for your safety?
> How were you able to ask your mum for help despite the doubt that your dad had planted about her being strong enough to cope with learning about the abuse?

Questions such as these enable the young person to see the situation from a different perspective that is premised on the harming father's accountability both for the sexual abuse and for undermining family relationships. They also acknowledge the child's courage and strength in resisting the abuse in courageous and creative ways.

## Rebuilding fractured relationships with the non-offending parent and siblings

As described throughout this book, a core tactic of the harming father is to undermine the mother–child relationship. Therapy must address this work to rebuild the mother–child bond. For this reason, mother–victim dyadic work is a key element of the approach, and is described in detail in Chapter 7. The types of questions outlined above can be particularly powerful in this dyadic work. For example, when secrecy is externalized as a key tactic by which the harming father concealed the abuse and disabled the mother's protective capacity, the effects on mother and daughter, both individually and on their relationship, can be explored together, giving new understanding for both of the tactics of division to which they have been subjected. For example, both may be asked:

> How has secrecy affected the ways in which your relationship has developed over the past few years?
> (To daughter) Were there any ways in which your step-dad encouraged secrecy?

## 82 Victimized children

(To mother) In what ways was your partner able to blind you with trickery about what he was doing?

Hearing each other respond to questions such as these exposes the role of the harming father in undermining their relationship. Similarly, hearing each other talk about their resistance to the tactics of abuse and division provides important information about the strengths of each and the strengths in their relationship.

While this approach can be used in all work with sexual assault survivors, an important benefit of the integrated Cedar Cottage approach is that additional information is available from the harming father's therapy about tactics which he has employed, about which either the victim, mother, or both would otherwise be unaware because of the very different sides of him that each separately experience. Additionally, in the case of children this can be due to their developmental level and for the mother, the degree of duplicity involved in his behaviour. As described in Chapter 3, the harming father is encouraged to face up to the ways in which he has set up, perpetrated and hidden his abusive behaviour and this information can be shared with other family members in a complex and well-prepared fashion as described in Chapter 7.

When women have been made aware of the ways in which they have been deceived, they are able to share the new understandings that flow from this with their daughters, opening the gate to a wealth of possibilities for talking about the effects on the mother–daughter relationship and also their hopes for it in the future. As one mother said, once the tactics of the abuse that were calculated to undermine her relationship with her daughter were known to her:

That hurt me more than the actual abuse. That hurts, that still hurts me, what he did to our relationship, how he manipulated both of us ... Once I realised how he went about it, how it was his fault that he did it and how he did do it, and the things he's put my daughter through as well, my God! Once I'd realised – my main aim was that my daughter and I get our relationship back again.

From her daughter's perspective:

We had a barrier between us, my mum and me, that my step-father built, and mum had to see him as the best thing made on earth and I had to see him as the best thing on earth, and maybe if I saw my mum or my mum saw me, we would start building a relationship that will be better between us than it would with him, like it will have nothing to do with him...

Another young woman described how she came to understand how the tactics the offender used to disempower her mother had blinded her mother to his sexual abuse of her:

> When I went to the program I realised how he was hiding it and how he was being so awful to my mum that she couldn't see anything, she could only see him because he was the main figure in the household, and everyone else just had to do things for him...

It is also important to attend to the relationship between the victimized child and her siblings. As argued in Chapter 6, siblings should be offered treatment in their own right, because of the impacts of incest and its disclosure on their family life. Additionally, intervention that provides them with accurate information about what has happened and about the harming father's responsibility is important as this can also play a role in the victimized child's recovery as the barriers erected between them are dismantled. For example, after disclosure of very long-term sexual abuse by her father, Elise suddenly changed from a quiet, compliant girl to an angry one who stayed out late drinking and who screamed abuse at her mother. Although her father had admitted to the abuse and had left the home, her behaviour became increasingly more challenging for her mother, who was at her wit's end. Her two brothers were furious with Elise for breaking up the family and for upsetting their mum, especially as their dad was doing all the 'right' things and getting therapy. When the superficiality of the father's apparent acceptance of responsibility was exposed and he made detailed disclosures to his wife about the tactics he had used both to abuse Elise and to perpetuate her isolation from the others in the family following disclosure, this new information that became available to the family was able to change her relationship with not only her mother but with her brothers.

> Yeah, well both of my brothers have both become aware of why I used to be such a little bitch. My oldest brother and I have become very close since the program because he's realised that. Now he's always inviting me out with his friends and I think he's realised that I'm not a pain.

Readers are referred to Chapter 7 where a detailed discussion is provided about the timing, nature and purpose of conjoint work within the Cedar Cottage model.

## Respecting and restoring the child's autonomy

Because sexual abuse involves complete disregard for the victimized child's wishes, all aspects of therapy need to attend to restoring the child's sense of control and autonomy. Work with the child emphasizes their right to make choices including: whether or not they wish to be involved in therapy with the agency that is also providing treatment to the harming father or with a separate agency; whether, and in what ways, they wish to participate in dyadic and family

## 84 Victimized children

sessions; whether and in what format they wish to receive information from the harming father's therapy that may support their recovery; and the nature of any future relationship with the harming father.

### When the victim is in therapy at another agency

In this situation, with the child and mother's permission, with regular communication between the therapeutic team, therapy consistent with the Cedar Cottage model can still be conducted. For example, the child may communicate via her therapist a list of questions that she has about the abuse to be considered by the harming father in the preparation for a letter or face-to-face session acknowledging his accountability. The child's therapist, whether external or internal to the program, always has the responsibility of advocating for the victim's wishes to be sought, heard and acted upon.

One possible disadvantage of the child's therapy being conducted at another agency is that there may be inconsistency in approaches. For example, therapists with expertise in working with victim/survivors may not be cognisant of the range of tactics of sexual abusers and in particular their ongoing deployment aimed at retaining their power in the family and undermining the development of therapeutic alliances for the mother or child. Sexual assault services may be using Trauma-Focussed Cognitive Behavioural Therapy (TF-CBT), which has been found to be effective in reducing many of the symptoms of Posttraumatic Stress Disorder (PTSD) and others such as anxiety and depression (Cohen, Deblinger, Mannarino, & Steer, 2004; Deblinger, Mannarino, Cohen, & Steer, 2006; Deblinger, Pollio, Runyon, & Steer, 2017). This approach involves a partnership with the parent and comprises a collection of core treatment components, including conjoint child–parent sessions to help the child and parent talk together about the child's trauma. Through liaison between the services, decisions can be made about which agency, or whether jointly, this aspect of the therapy – which is central to the Cedar Cottage model – is most usefully conducted. For example the mother and child's therapy including dyadic sessions may occur at the agency working with the victim, but informed by the mother's participation in sessions at Cedar Cottage in which her partner faces up to the ways in which he planned, initiated and hid the sexual abuse.

### Safe recontact with the harming father?

As discussed earlier in this book, the Cedar Cottage Program required the harming father entering the program to live apart from the family and to have no contact with the victimized child and other children in the family until approved by the program. This attended to the risks of further sexual abuse and of the harming father pressuring the child to recant or forgive, or mobilizing the mother and siblings in support of his version of events to further isolate the victimized child. This sets the scene for the program to take an active role in structuring therapy so that the central concern is always the safety, well-being and autonomy of the victim/s.

Sexually victimized children can be expected to have a range of perspectives on whether, or to what extent, they wish to have contact with the harming father, even if his progress in therapy indicates that this is possible. Some, more often in the case of biological fathers, may wish to have their father demonstrate his accountability for the harm he has caused, and to rebuild a relationship of some kind with him. Others may want little or nothing to do with him and may be indifferent to hearing his account of his behaviour. Unlike earlier approaches to this issue, where children were expected to accede to the decisions about these matters made by the parents (Giaretto, 1982), the Cedar Cottage Program was clear that the choices of the victimized child must be respected by the therapeutic team. At the same time, these choices can be explored supportively in order to see if the child is being pressured by family members to adopt a certain position, for example, experiencing pressure to accept a premature apology as a path to family reunification or acting out of loyalty to put other family members' wishes and needs ahead of her own in a pattern established during the sexual abuse.

### Preparing the child for the harming father's 'facing up'

When the child wishes to have the harming father take responsibility for the abuse and harm caused through participating in a 'facing up' process, careful and thorough preparation work with the child is essential to ensure that the experience is safe and in the interest of her recovery. This work proceeds over several sessions and involves a number of steps. In the first session it is important to provide the child with information about the face-up process, and to address any concerns or worries she may have about the process. The child then works with her therapist to prepare her goals of meeting with the harming father, recorded as 'what I want to get out of the meeting and what I see as its purpose'. She is then invited to generate a list of tactics used by her father. Only after this preparation does the child receive the written face-up information that the offender has prepared in his therapy. The written face-up may be provided to older children prior to the information being made available to the mother, while for younger victims, the mother may receive the information prior to it being passed on to the victim in order that the mother determine the appropriateness of the victim receiving the face-up material and having a face-to-face meeting.

This leads to a discussion in this and subsequent sessions about the extent to which the content of the face-up fits with the child's experience of the abuse; whether there are any gaps in what the offender has acknowledged; and whether she is left with any questions about what has been said in the face-up. In response to the face-up material, the child generates a list of questions for the offender, which are recorded as 'Questions I have for ......' Children in the program have had questions such as: 'Did you really care about me?' 'Why me?' 'You said I could say "no", but when I did say "no" why did you keep going?' Other questions involved the child finding out information that potentially affected their other relationships, such as: 'Have you told mum everything?'

Further preparation for a face-to-face meeting involves the child identifying the things that happen for them when they are anxious, angry, upset etc. They discuss their usual ways of coping with difficult feelings and plan how they will manage these in the meeting, and how they will indicate to their therapist that they need assistance, such as stopping for a break.

The child also develops and documents lists relating to: things she doesn't want to see happen; things to look out for that tell her that her parent has changed; her expectations of the meeting; and how she will know whether they have been met. She is invited to discuss the impact the abuse has had on her life and significant relationships. This can be important in terms of preparing the child to assess whether her father provides her with information that comes close to appreciating the harm and impact caused by his abusive actions.

The standards that the harming father has prepared for his conduct in the meeting are also made available to the child so that she can ask questions or raise concerns about these. Self-care is addressed and planned for, with the child encouraged to anticipate how she will look after herself before, during and after the face-up meeting and to identify support people in her network.

An advantage of the Cedar Cottage model is that the harming father is required to be accountable to those he has harmed and to be transparent and honest about his behaviours. In his therapy, he is held to the highest standards of honesty in responding to the victim's questions and is unable to respond with glib apologies or in ways that invite pity for his situation or which shift responsibility onto others. The ways in which communication with the harming father during the face-up session is carefully planned, structured and conducted is discussed in detail in Chapter 7.

The ways in which the harming father addresses the child's questions can provide her with information which informs her decisions about the type of future contact she wants with him. For example, on completing the program that involved the harming father facing up to her, one girl said: 'I never thought that he'd take responsibility for what he'd done actually, but he did.' She wanted an ongoing relationship with her biological father and supported his return to the home. Through the therapy with her mother, she also saw that the power balance had changed and that her mother was stronger: 'She's much more her own person now whereas when Dad was home she sort of did whatever Dad said, she's like, got her own personality now.'

In contrast, another young woman found her step-father's facing up lacking in genuine empathy for the harm he had caused. She was angry about his sense of entitlement about the family reunification towards which they were working and subsequently spoke out against his return to the family, and was supported in this decision by her mother.

> He knows how it's hurt people, but he doesn't know the feeling of hurt, like he's cried and everything to my mum and me, but it doesn't mean anything, it doesn't change anything. We're giving him a really big chance (to return to the home) and I don't think he accepts it, well he accepts it but he doesn't feel really grateful, like he thinks, 'Oh, they should have done it anyway.'

## Conclusion

Work with victimized children aims to help them to unravel the effects of secrecy, mis-placed responsibility and manipulated loyalty on themselves and on their relationships, to rebuild relationships with their mother and siblings and to restore a sense of control, courage and autonomy. When the goals of therapy were achieved, young women spoke of the outcomes of therapy in the following terms:

> It helped me by making me realize it's not my fault, and they helped with mum and my relationship. (Katie)
> Well, after a long time you get to have your self-respect back, and you just become a person again, which you trust and you get connected to your feelings, like you agree with, kind of thing, and you don't have to feel pressured into anything, and it makes you feel better and then once you get yourself better you can talk to other people and sort that relationship out. (Amy)

## References

Alaggia, R., Collin-Vézina, D., & Lateef, R. (2017). Facilitators and barriers to child sexual abuse (CSA) disclosures. *Trauma, Violence, & Abuse, 0*(0), 1524838017697312. doi:10.1177/1524838017697312

Berliner, L., & Conte, J. R. (1990). The process of victimization: The victims' perspective. *Child Abuse and Neglect, 14*(1), 29–40.

Christiansen, J. R., & Blake, R. H. (1990). The grooming process in father–daughter incest. In A. L. Horton (Ed.), *The Incest Perpetrator: A Family Member No One Wants to Treat* (pp. 88–98). Thousand Oaks, CA: Sage Publications.

Cohen, J. A., Deblinger, E., Mannarino, A. P., & Steer, R. A. (2004). A multisite, randomized controlled trial for children with sexual abuse-related PTSD symptoms. *Journal of the American Academy of Child and Adolescent Psychiatry, 43*(4), 393–402.

Deblinger, E., Mannarino, A. P., Cohen, J. A., & Steer, R. A. (2006). A follow-up study of a multisite, randomized, controlled trial for children with sexual abuse-related PTSD symptoms. *Journal of the American Academy of Child and Adolescent Psychiatry, 45*(12), 1474–1484.

Deblinger, E., Pollio, E., Runyon, M. K., & Steer, R. A. (2017). Improvements in personal resiliency among youth who have completed trauma-focused cognitive behavioral therapy: A preliminary examination. *Child Abuse & Neglect, 65*, 132–139. doi:10.1016/j.chiabu.2016.12.014

Dupont, M., Messerschmitt, P., Vila, G., Bohu, D., & Rey-Salmon, C. (2014). The disclosure of extrafamily and intrafamily child sexual abuse. *Annales Medico-Psychologiques, 172*(6), 426–431. doi:10.1016/j.amp.2012.06.024

Giaretto, H. (1982). *Integrated Treatment of Child Sexual Abuse*. Palo Alto: Science and Behaviour Books, Inc.

Goetzold, S. (2017). An open and shut case of closed questions: An exploration of joint investigative interview training in Scotland. *Child Abuse Review, 26*(2), 116–129. doi:10.1002/car.2391

Goodman-Brown, T. B., Edelstein, R. S., Goodman, G. S., Jones, D. P. H., & Gordon, D. S. (2003). Why children tell: A model of children's disclosure of sexual abuse. *Child Abuse & Neglect, 27*(5), 525–540. doi:10.1016/s0145-2134(03)00037-1

Laing, L., & Kamsler, A. (1990). Putting an end to secrecy: Therapy with mothers and children following disclosure of child sexual assault. In M. Durrant & C. White (Eds.), *Ideas for Therapy with Sexual Abuse* (pp. 159–181). Adelaide, S.A.: Dulwich Centre Publications.

Leach, C., Powell, M. B., Sharman, S. J., & Anglim, J. (2017). The relationship between children's age and disclosures of sexual abuse during forensic interviews. *Child Maltreatment, 22*(1), 79–88. doi:10.1177/1077559516675723

London, K., Bruck, M., Ceci, S. J., & Shuman, D. W. (2005). Disclosure of child sexual abuse: What does the research tell us about the ways that children tell? *Psychology Public Policy and Law, 11*(1), 194–226.

McElvaney, R., & Culhane, M. (2017). A retrospective analysis of children's assessment reports: What helps children tell? *Child Abuse Review, 26*(2), 103–115. doi:10.1002/car.2390

Phelan, P. (1995). Incest and its meaning: The perspectives of fathers and daughters. *Child Abuse and Neglect, 19*(1), 7–24.

Staller, K. M., & Nelson-Gardell, D. (2005). "A burden in your heart": Lessons of disclosure from female preadolescent and adolescent survivors of sexual abuse. *Child Abuse & Neglect, 29*, 1415–1432.

Summit, R. (1983). The child abuse accommodation syndrome. *Child Abuse and Neglect, 7*(2), 177–193.

Wade, A. (1997). Small acts of living: Everyday resistance to violence and other forms of oppression. *Contemporary Family Therapy, 19*(1), 23–39.

White, M. (2007). *Maps of Narrative Practice*. New York: W. W. Norton and Company.

White, M., & Epston, D. (1989). *Literate Means to Therapeutic Ends*. Adelaide: Dulwich Centre Publications.

# Chapter 6

# Siblings

## Introduction

Siblings of the sexually victimized child experience profound changes in their family when parental child sexual abuse is discovered. The crisis of discovery and the ensuing fallout affect them deeply, warranting intervention for this group in their own right. Siblings are also central to supporting the victimized child's recovery.

Little has been written about working with siblings after child sexual assault, and they are often invisible in discussions about it. This invisibility reflects a general neglect of sibling relationships in the social sciences, despite a growing body of literature establishing their importance in cognitive, emotional and social development, resilience and navigation of adolescence and adult relationships (Caffaro, 2014). For example, it has been established that by age four, second-born children spend more time talking to and playing with their older siblings than with their parents (Dunn, 1993 in Caffaro, 2014). In adolescence and young adulthood, these relationships continue to be central, being independent predictors for later depression and emotional well-being (Vaillant & Vaillant, 1990 and Wadlinger et al., in Caffaro, 2014).

Incest is a betrayal of all family member's primary relationships (Sheinberg & Fraenkel, 2001). It disrupts the relational skills for which sibling relationships are foundational, and as a result, children's overall development. Equally, where supportive relationships exist between the abused child and their siblings, these may be protective, promoting greater resilience.

A further consideration for siblings is the impact of the co-occurrence of parental child sexual abuse and other forms of intra-familial violence, which were outlined in Chapter 1. As well as impacting on the victimized child/ren, the siblings may have grown up in a climate of coercion, isolation and secrecy. Children who observe domestic violence often experience a high rate of emotional and/or behavioural difficulties themselves (Gartland et al., 2014), further highlighting the value of intervention with siblings in their own right.

## The crisis of disclosure/discovery

Disclosure or discovery of the abuse is a profound crisis for the whole family and a time of extreme anxiety for the siblings. They may experience overwhelming anger, guilt and fear. Although siblings are less commonly aware of what has been occurring and may be wholly unprepared for it, the discovery disrupts their understanding of their own and their family's identity. Police investigation, court processes or removal of the harming father or their victimized sibling, bring significant shame and stigma. Commonly siblings face denial by the harming father, a partial account from their mother – often limited in detail in order to protect them, and differing accounts from others. This leaves the siblings swirling in competing stories and looking for someone to blame for upending their lives. In sifting competing accounts, the siblings often accept the harming father's denial. After all, it is their father who has typically been the most powerful person in the family and whose views and directions have prevailed. Believing their sister can place siblings in an incongruent position of loving and needing a parent while acknowledging a major flaw (Baker, Tanis, & Rice, 2002). As a result, their sister's disclosure is often disbelieved. Most commonly they blame her, and are angry with her for creating problems for the harming father, if not for breaking up the family. This can be extremely distressing for the victimized child, who has often been prompted to disclose the abuse to protect her younger siblings from the same fate.

In some instances, siblings align quickly with the victimized child but subsequently become critical of her and disconnect if she expresses anything other than anger and disapproval towards the harming father. This alignment is more likely to occur where the harming father has also been physically abusive towards the mother or other children in the family. These initial reactions can change rapidly as the crisis escalates and others become involved or informed, such as statutory agencies. An arrest or public awareness about the assaults is likely to be experienced by siblings as humiliating and stigmatizing, for which the victimized child is often blamed, particularly if the harming father is arrested or removed from the home. Fear and confusion sown in these circumstances are most easily directed at their sibling, rather than at the powerful, and often charismatic figure of the father in the family. Such negative reactions are rendered even more likely when siblings have been distanced from the victimized child through the prior tactics of the offender.

As outlined in Chapter 3, the tactics of the harming father, precede, accompany and continue after the abuse of a child is discovered. For this reason, therapeutic work needs to take account of the likelihood that new tactics may be directed at the siblings, as a means of undermining their belief in the disclosure or support for their sister. The harming father may also be engaging in covert communication which is beyond the awareness of the therapist or mother.

## Experiences of siblings in relation to the harming father's tactics

Tactics directed to the siblings are undertaken for a different purpose to those directed against the harmed child, though often similar to those directed towards the mother. Chief among the purposes of these tactics are discrediting, isolating or marginalizing the victimized child. By creating distance between the victimized child and her siblings, sources of support and belief for her are reduced, as are opportunities for safe disclosure.

> Drew sexually assaulted his daughter Stephanie aged 14 and over many years treated her quite differently to her younger siblings, Jackson (12), Amy (10) and Troy (8). Using her status as oldest child as a pretext, he endowed her with freedoms and gifts disproportionately more generous than those afforded to the other children. This included: renovating the garage to create a room of Stephanie's own, while the younger children all shared the same bedroom; taking her on extra outings; and buying her coveted brand name clothes. In fact these privileges all provided greater opportunities for Drew to assault Stephanie, but also sowed resentment among the younger children, creating a wedge between them.

Tactics directed towards siblings may also be undertaken by the harming father to set up a new victim of abuse. It is often discovery of grooming of another sibling that leads victimized children to disclose their abuse.

## Responding to disclosures by siblings of further sexual assaults

An issue requiring careful consideration is the possibility that other children in the family have also been sexually harmed by the father. In consideration of specific risk factors for incest offenders, Proeve (2009) identified from earlier studies that multiple female children are abused in 15 per cent of cases of father–daughter incest, with probable sexual approaches to female siblings of a sexually abused daughter in more than 50 per cent of cases. In relation to boys, who are identified victims of sexual abuse by their fathers, additional victims are identified in 60 per cent of cases (usually the boys' sisters). This indicates that multiple victims in a family are not uncommon, particularly where boys have been targeted. Despite the commonality of multiple victims, it is typical that the children are unaware of one another's abuse.

It cannot be assumed that a disclosure will prompt other victims in the family to report their own experiences of abuse. If a first child who discloses encounters disbelief, blame or other forms of scapegoating, other children may be deterred from speaking up. Subsequent disclosures by siblings are not uncommon, particularly in circumstances where belief and support attend the initial child's disclosure. Alternatively further victimized children may be identified through additional admissions by the harming father. In such instances the mother and identified child must be informed and official reports including statutory child protection reports made. In circumstances such as these, careful attention must be paid to the needs of the child about whom a disclosure is made, in order that they are not further traumatized or experience the disclosure as further deprivation of their choice and control. It is important to move slowly and with deliberation, ensuring that the harming father is encouraged to take responsibility for the abuse and to consider how this further admission may be received by the child and mother.

> Rick was attending treatment for assaulting his step-daughter Phoebe (10) who had disclosed the abuse to her gym teacher. In the course of treatment and adding to Phoebe's account of her abuse, he made further admissions to having had sexually explicit conversations with her brother Jamie (12) which included Rick offering to suck Jamie's penis 'so Jamie could see what it felt like'. Jamie denied any occurrence of this when it was gently raised in a counselling session with him by one of the team members and has continued to say that this didn't happen. This response was most likely a result of Jamie's embarrassment and shame and perhaps also a response to what Jamie saw as the catastrophic impact on the family of Phoebe's disclosure.

## Needs and role of siblings in therapeutic work

The primary purpose of work with siblings is to break down the shame and isolation that parental child sexual abuse brings to the harmed child and re-build enduring, protective relationships between the child and her siblings. In doing this work, the harms to the siblings and their own unique needs are not overlooked. Although it can be tempting to remain focussed on the mother and victimized child or harming father, attention to siblings should follow rapidly. It is important too, not to leave this work to the mother in a misplaced attempt to shore up her authority. The significance of the sibling relationships to the victimized child warrants that they are explicitly involved in therapy. A first need of siblings in therapeutic work is for information, in order that they may understand the nature of their father's behaviour, his tactics and how this has impacted on all the relationships in the family. Many families keep the abuse hidden from siblings, thinking that this information may be too painful for children to hear (Baker et al., 2002). Unless the developmental range of the siblings indicates otherwise, this work is usefully done as a sibling group. The mother is also usually present, to reinforce her leadership of the family unit and prevent the creation of further divisions. The inclusion of the victimized child in these conversations is not necessary, as she may be further burdened by having to take responsibility for her siblings' needs, though she should be consulted about what is said about her experiences and attend if she expresses this as a preference. The initial approach taken with siblings involves careful exploration of four questions in turn as follows.

## What do you know?

Make no assumptions about what the siblings know about the assaults. Disbelief, followed by blame towards the victimized child, are predictable, but also typically based on a lack of information, or deliberate mis-information provided by the harming father or others acting to protect him. This first critical step involves carefully exploring with the siblings, what they know, believe or assume and the sources of this information. Planning this session in advance with the mother, allows decisions to be made about what corrective information the siblings should be given and by whom. Information needs to be at the siblings' developmental level, balancing concerns of others in the family about privacy, particularly the victimized child, considering issues of shame and the impact of sharing details of specific sexual acts. Whether she wishes to be involved or not, prior consultation with the victimized child is essential in order to assist in restoring her sense of control. The planning will also address how information is conveyed in such a way that the mother is not undermined in her parenting role.

This conversation also provides space to hear from the siblings how they have been affected by the disclosure and to acknowledge the distress and ongoing impacts on them, in a forum where neither the mother nor victimized child is burdened. Discussion can also include what questions the siblings have of the harming father and how they would like these to be conveyed to him. Examples of useful questions are:

> What do you understand has happened in the family which means that Dad isn't living at home anymore?
>
> What have you been told about what happened between Tracy and your father?
>
> What would you like to ask your Dad about this if you had the chance? How would you like these questions passed on to him?

## What do you believe?

A second and separate element of this conversation is to establish what the sibling/s believe to be the accurate version of events. Inevitably the siblings have been exposed to competing 'truths', termed by Anna Salter, a 'battle of realities' (Salter, 1995, p. 120). Versions of events may have been traded between the siblings, unknown to the mother, no matter how concerned and involved she is with her children. This conversation provides space to acknowledge the likelihood of these competing truths and the difficulty for the siblings of determining whose truth to accept. Siblings rarely at this point have been given an opportunity to understand what has occurred and process it. New knowledge brings new feelings and the siblings can be invited to re-consider the meaning of what has occurred in light of new knowledge. So if for example, Stephanie has for years been suffering their father's abuse, perhaps she is not the spoilt brat or uppity teenager that their father has encouraged them to see, but a wronged sister who has suffered injustice. It can be useful for siblings to consider the time sequence of how they came to see things in certain ways and the role of the harming father in shaping their perceptions and relationships. This then opens space for them to consider how this changes meanings and the feelings which attach to them. For example:

> I guess you might have heard different things about what happened and who's to blame... and it's pretty hard to know who is right. What do *you* think happened?
>
> You have probably heard different versions of events. Which one at the moment do you think is right? What's swaying you that way?
>
> Where does that information come from?
>
> When did you first get that impression of your sister? How did that come about?
>
> What difference does it make now to know that during that time he was hurting her, she was keeping your dad's secret?

### Have you conveyed that to your sister?

Working carefully to avoid further circles of blame, the therapist reviews with the siblings what they have communicated so far to their sister in relation to the abuse. Both verbal and non-verbal messages are considered. Subtle and less subtle anger and blame are likely, but need to be acknowledged in order for the siblings to identify the need for different messages to be conveyed. Place in family and age of siblings in relation to each other, will shape both what is told to the child/ren and also their likely influence on the harmed child. Older siblings who are still living at home may be able to be given more information as is developmentally appropriate and in most cases are also in a stronger position to have a positive influence on shifting the blame away from the harmed child, which is a significant step in re-building the sibling relationships. They are also well placed to play an overall role in the re-storying in the family of the abuse.

> What do you think your sister thinks you believe? What might that be like for her?
>
> What sort of impact do you think your dad's actions, and the reaction when it came out, might have had on her?

What sort of things have you said to her about this situation since it first came out in the open?

What kind of impressions is that likely to have left her with?

What sort of things do you think it could be helpful for her to hear from other members of the family now?

### Have you communicated to your sister that you are aware of the impact on her?

Supported to believe in their sister's account, and the reality of her experience of abuse, the siblings can then consider what she needs to hear from them and what they might say to her. Hearing from each of them that she is believed and not blamed for bringing distress to their mother, any adverse outcomes they are individually experiencing or for what may be the break-up of the family, is important for her recovery and for re-building the family connections.

In the light of what you now know to be the case, is there something you think she'd appreciate hearing from you?

Thinking about it now, is there something that you would want to let her know?

What kind of difference might hearing that from you make for her?

## Additional therapeutic issues

Some siblings face unique challenges in this process. Children for whom the harming father's tactics of division have strongly alienated the children from the victimized child may have taken on 'accomplice' roles for which they harbour a strong sense of guilt. Some children, for example, have been recruited to help the abuser monitor and restrict the actions of the victimized child (Baker et al., 2002).

Writing in the context of adolescent sibling sexual assault, psychologist John Caffaro (2014, pp. 181–184), notes that including non-abusive siblings in conjoint work with a victimized child can be productive in a number of ways. These include: acting as valuable consultants to the therapist or harmed child through additional perspectives on family history; loosening an outdated, frozen reputation of their sister; opening up space for the other to acknowledge certain events or perspectives; or modelling different types of behaviour, such as assertiveness/expression of feelings. Caffaro also notes the particular importance of work to re-build sibling relationships when parents are unable to care for them. With parental child sexual abuse, this work becomes even more important when the relationship between the mother and victimized child remains fractured.

Brothers of girls abused by their fathers may have specific needs which can be addressed through sibling work. Often identifying closely with their father, they may feel particular shame or have adopted norms of masculinity and entitlement. Describing therapeutic work with boys after a sibling has experienced parental child sexual abuse, Hill (2003) notes the deeply rooted cultural belief that character is both inherited from the father and is related to destiny; this can significantly impact on the development of boys' sense of masculine identity, sowing fears that they too will become 'perverts'. At Cedar Cottage, we found that with supportive intervention many of these boys were able to take a stand against male entitlement and convey to their sisters a different model of masculinity, based on respect towards girls and women. Such a stance is very useful in the victimized child's therapy.

A further important piece of work with siblings after parental child sexual abuse, which Sheinberg and Fraenkel (2001) identify, involves creating a space for them (as for the victimized child) to discuss their enduring loyalties to the harming father, while at the same time re-shaping the boundaries to maximise safety.

Much of the therapeutic intervention in which siblings are involved is likely to be conjoint work, with the victimized child, mother and potentially the harming father. Conversations between the mother and the siblings and victimized child/ren allow these fractured relationships to be rebuilt. The purpose, timing and issues for consideration in conjoint work are further addressed in Chapter 7.

### *Loss of connection to the extended family*

An unanticipated, but nonetheless significant impact on siblings is that they often lose contact with the harming father's family, the children's grandparents, aunts, uncles and cousins. In some cultures more than others, this loss is dramatic as well as socially stigmatizing. The harming father's own parents and family are in most instances drawn into and accepting of his explanation of the disclosure, which may include outright denial, minimization and blame shifting. Under these circumstances continued contact with the victimized child and siblings is untenable. Even those extended family members who choose to believe the child will usually, from loyalty alone, act to support the harming father, which is often incompatible with remaining in supportive contact. There are exceptions to this with some extended family members, actively preserving relationships, for example between cousins.

Working with the harming father's family, including his parents, is of great value, not only to create witnesses to his risk factors into the future, but also to rebuild these relationships, which can be of significant importance to the victimized child and her siblings. This is further addressed in Chapters 8 and 9.

## Safe re-contact with the harming father

A consistent rule at Cedar Cottage was that the harming father had no contact with either the victimized child or any of the siblings at the outset of treatment.

This stance was taken to prevent divisions, employment of further tactics and also because of the potential that any of them are unidentified victims. It is consistent with the victim-centred approach to assign higher priority to the sibling relationship, than to the relationship between the non-abused siblings and harming father.

Safe re-contact for siblings has several dimensions. Firstly, the harming father must have admitted to the assaults in full, providing a more complete account than that given in the disclosure by the identified abused child. The second dimension is that the siblings need to be informed – to the extent that is developmentally appropriate – of their father's abusive actions, as outlined above. Even when this has occurred they will continue to be highly subject to manipulation by him of both the truth and their loyalties.

A first re-contact with the harming father occurs in the therapeutic setting at the point when the harming father is ready to face up to the children in relation to his actions and so continue the important work of taking responsibility for the harms he has done. This process should not happen too early in the therapeutic work as it requires the harming father to do considerable preparation, taking into account and addressing his tactics towards them, their developmental stage/s, and what he may need to tell them in relation to his tactics towards their mother. Facilitating this process is a complex therapeutic intervention, which may include addressing impatience by the mother and siblings for this to happen early. If undertaken too early and without appropriate preparation, the harming father will be likely to attempt to use this session to continue to impose his 'truth' or to draw the focus of sympathy back to himself.

If ongoing contact is agreed to between the harming father and siblings, it is likely that he will propose special outings such as picnics, which will have high appeal. Consideration needs to be given to what plans are made for the victimized child during such events. We have found that it is not uncommon for her to be left out in such a way that leaves her feeling ostracized rather than protected and reinforces the divisions in the family.

Unsupervised contact with the harming father should not occur when any of the children are of a developmental stage which makes them a likely target of abuse. The siblings need to understand not only his past behaviour but the ongoing risks posed by him in relation to further child sexual assault, so that they are aware into the future of risks to leaving any other children – including at some point potentially their own children, in his care.

## Conclusion

Forging enduring safety for children after parental child sexual abuse must include involvement in therapy of the siblings of the victim and also the harming father's children from other relationships (further addressed in Chapter 8). Until all of the harming father's children and step-children are informed – by him – of his actions, they are vulnerable to distorted views of him, the victimized child and their mother. They are also potentially vulnerable to sexual abuse or to unwittingly facilitating access to other potential victims. Siblings can be a critical part of creating safety for the victimized child as well as contributing significantly to her recovery.

In the next chapter we consider the needs of extended family members, including non-offending fathers, those biological or step-parents who have not themselves sexually assaulted their daughters but whose relationships with them have also been damaged by the assaults.

## References

Baker, J. N., Tanis, H. J., & Rice, J. B. (2002). Including siblings in the treatment of child sexual abuse. *Journal of Child Sexual Abuse, 10*(3), 1–16. doi:10.1300/J070v10n03_01

Caffaro, J. (2014). *Sibling Abuse Trauma: Assessment and Intervention Strategies for Children, Families and Adults* (2nd ed.). New York: Routledge

Gartland, D., Woolhouse, H., Mensah, F., Hegarty, K., Hiscock, H., & Brown, S. (2014). The case for early intervention to reduce the impact of intimate partner abuse on child outcomes: Results of an Australian cohort of first-time mothers. *Birth, 41*(4), 374–383.

Hill, A. (2003). Issues facing brothers of sexually abused children: Implications for professional practice. *Child & Family Social Work*, 8(4), 281–290.

Proeve, M. (2009). A preliminary examination of specific risk assessment for sexual offenders against children. *Journal of Child Sexual Abuse, 18*(6), 583–593. doi:10.1080/10926770903307898

Salter, A. (1995). *Transforming Trauma: A Guide to Understanding and Treating Adult Survivors of Child Sexual Abuse*. Newbury Park, CA: Sage Publications.

Sheinberg, M., & Fraenkel, P. (2001). *The Relational Trauma of Incest: A Family Based Approach to Treatment*. New York: The Guilford Press.

# Chapter 7

# Conjoint work within an integrated approach to therapy

## Integrated treatment

The Cedar Cottage approach is an integrated treatment model in which therapeutic work with the harming father is integrated with that of the victimized child, her siblings, her mother and other members of the extended family.

Integrated treatment involves understanding and connecting the individual's goals of treatment with the therapeutic processes of others. For example, a mother is likely to have multiple information needs, which are pivotal to her own and others' recovery, such as details of how her child was sexually abused. One source of information is the victimized child but questioning her daughter about this can be very problematic. Often the mother–daughter relationship is conflictual, due to the divisive tactics of the harming father. Further, there are also details of the abuse of which the child will not be aware, for example the harming father's planning of the abuse. An alternate source of information is the harming father. Ideally in his individual therapy he has set goals of being honest, volunteering information and responding to questions about his sexual abuse of the child. This is one way in which he can begin to demonstrate acceptance of responsibility. The information he shares about how he set up and carried out the sexual abuse can be critical to the mother gaining a new understanding of her child's experience, which can in turn influence her response to her child. The information he provides also enables the mother to assess her partner's (or former partner's) response against standards of accountability as well as to make sense for herself of the expanding description of the abuse, which is now likely to be very different to the initial information that was available to her. The mother's complex information needs include: the frequency of the sexual abuse and acts involved; how the harming father set up the abuse, carried it out and acted to prevent disclosure; how he was able to engage in multiple layers of relationship as a partner and a parent (*at the time of sexually abusing the child*) and significantly, his current thoughts, beliefs, focus and goals. This is an ongoing assessment and re-assessment. Is he still conducting himself in self-centred ways, focussed on self-protection and acting to manipulate others around his beliefs and self-interest?

## The role of conjoint work within integrated treatment

It is important to distinguish integrated from conjoint therapy. Conjoint work is relational and involves dyads or groups (including whole families) in the same sessions, working to shared objectives. Integrated treatment may or may not include conjoint work. Importantly, integrated treatment does not presume that conjoint work is appropriate; nor is conjoint work an indicator of integration. In some cases, an expectation of conjoint work can in fact be harmful. An example is an expectation that a child who has been sexually abused by a parent should agree to participate in conjoint therapy with the parent, or that a child not agreeing to do so indicates a deficit of some kind in the child's recovery.

The context in which therapeutic responses are being delivered will influence the possibility for integrated or conjoint work. Conjoint work is regarded as essential for several of the family dyads, the most significant being the mother–daughter dyad. Other essential dyads are mother with harming father and mother with sibling/s and victimized child.

Work with the harming father and victimized child is always integrated. For example, whatever the victim's stance about receiving information from the harming father's therapy, he is encouraged to work in his therapy to be transparent about his abusive behaviours and tactics as an indication of his commitment to contributing to her recovery. Likewise, the child's therapist will explore with her whether she has any questions for her father. However, the child should never be compelled to participate in any form of communication with the harming father unless she chooses to do this, has control over the ways in which this will happen and has preparatory sessions as outlined in Chapter 5. If conjoint work between the harming father and the victimized child does occur, this occurs in the later stages of the harming father's therapy, when he has reached a point of maturation through his therapy, and only after significant preparation on the part of all family members. It should not happen in the early stages of the family's therapy. The safety of the child is the prime concern and any conjoint work needs to manage the risk of re-traumatizing the child.

The significance of timing and sequencing of individual and conjoint work after child sexual assault has been identified elsewhere (Sheinberg & Fraenkel, 2001). Ideally each family member has access to a therapist to ensure that conjoint work is carefully planned as part of the therapeutic process for each person, with good communication across the therapeutic team. All dyad work requires individual preparation including anticipation of the experience of being part of a joint process. While there is not a fixed order in which dyad work should take place, harming father–victim dyad should follow individual and other dyad work, especially victim–mother dyad.

A key therapeutic process in the harming father's therapy and steps to remediation is the 'face-up' meeting. This is a process of acknowledgement by the harming father, which is not an apology but refers to a thoughtful, prepared statement in which he outlines in detail, how he committed the abuses including planning and the use of tactics and takes responsibility for his actions. The application of the concept of facing up in this area was based on work by Alan Jenkins (1990) who applied it originally to work with men who used violence against their partners.

## Conjoint work

### Harming father–mother (parent dyad)

Early parent dyad work is possible but careful support and direction is required. The needs of the adults may be intense and if not managed well attention to this dyad may be at the expense of the child or children. There is a risk that the harming father will try to use this as an opportunity to try to engage in 'proving' himself, and engage the mother in focussing on *his* difficulties, *his* emotional reaction to disclosure or *his* positive qualities including *his* love and commitment to her. Effective preparation for the conjoint work engages him instead in seeking to 'prove' himself by committing himself to facing and acknowledging the full extent of his actions, their consequences and doing whatever he can to facilitate healing and recovery of others. Consistent with his commitment to being honest and accountable, how thoroughly he applies himself to these matters can be evaluated by the mother.

The first step in this process involves separate preparatory sessions. Preparation includes deciding whether, and if so, how both parents would like to communicate with each other or meet face-to-face. However, planning is not a joint process as may be the case in much relationship counselling because the relationship is understood as unequal. Without separate planning the mother may be disadvantaged and the process itself misunderstood to be a negotiation, which it is not. The process is a forum in which the harming father gives information and responds to questions and the mother receives information and evaluates the content and qualities of the interaction for the purpose of her recovery and healing.

The first face-up meeting of parent dyads can begin with the harming father committing to taking responsibility including:

1    Providing a clear account to the mother of the sexual abuse including his actions, words used, steps taken to set up the sexual abuse and carry it out, and how he prevented earlier disclosure.
2    Acknowledging ways he denied or minimized his sexually abusive behaviour, including by omission (saying 'only so much' at a time).
3    Refraining from offering explanations for his actions and not joining, managing or co-processing the information.

## 102 Conjoint work

Typically, the mother is not aware of the details of the sexual abuse in the early stages after disclosure, at which time if a police report has been made, the harming father has faced an official investigation by police and/or the statutory child protection agency. He may have made admissions about the sexual abuse. An investigation process typically begins with interview of the child and other witnesses. This is followed by an interview with the harming father in which the matters confirmed by the investigation are put to him as allegations. In this context his initial responses can be measured against the allegations and if his responses meet the allegations, they rarely exceed them. Mothers may be given an outline of the harming father's responses but not the details. It may not be until later when the matter is before a Court that the detail of his responses becomes known to her. The mother may have been instructed by the prosecutor or child protection authorities not to discuss details with the harming father, or with the child. Generally by the time a therapeutic process is being undertaken, the harming father has provided a narrative to the mother and possibly significant others such as grandparents. This narrative rarely provides comprehensive details of the sexual abuse.

A first step in preparing the mother for parent dyad work is to review in her therapy what she knows about the abuse and the source(s) of that information. Checking with her if she would like a clear outline from the harming father can be paralleled in the father's therapy by his therapist inviting him to prepare a description of his actions, including his planning to sexually abuse. This may occupy a number of sessions.

As discussed at the start of this chapter, hearing her partner's detailed account about how he orchestrated the abuse and enforced secrecy can contribute to the mother's belief and support of the child. It also provides the opportunity for her to review with her therapist what the harming father has previously told her or left her to believe. This process also relieves the child of having to re-tell what she may experience at this stage as shameful.

The beginning step in preparation for this face-up meeting by the harming father is to review with his therapist the initial proposed acknowledgment (account) that he has prepared for the mother as it may contain mixed messages of responsibility, include minimization or denial and focus on himself. Preparing this initial account is set as a written task for the harming father. In the earlier stages of the Cedar Cottage Program, this took the form of a letter from the harming father to the mother. Due to repeated experiences of harming fathers using a letter format as an opportunity for attempting to manipulate their partners, the account was separated from letter or direct person-to-person communication. A typical example of a harming father attempting to use the letter format in this ways is:

> Please do not doubt that I ever stopped loving you. This is the greatest shame I will ever have to bear. I feel sick thinking about you having to read this ...

Rather than providing information to help the mother have direct confirmation of what the harming father has done, to help her believe and respond to her daughter and make sense of this for herself, the harming father in this example begins by focussing attention on himself and the connection between them. In this way he is attempting to position the mother emotionally to limit her negative response to him.

During assessment harming fathers are asked to acknowledge their actions by providing a 'Crime Description'. This task commonly evokes a strong reaction as it explicitly recognizes the criminality of the sexual abuse, a matter which the harming father at this stage usually does not acknowledge. Similarly the concept of planning sexual abuse is challenging as most harming fathers initially present their sexually abusive actions as impulsive, outside of their control and possibly initiated by the victim. The therapist can open the process of identifying planning by asking the harming father when he first thought about or noticed the child in a sexual way. If the harming father identifies doing this, the therapist can then ask when this changed from noticing to deciding to act. This could be days or minutes ahead of sexually abusing. An account by the harming father that includes details of his forethought and planning, in addition to the sexual abuse behaviours, provides the mother with very important, new information.

If the harming father does not have literacy skills to complete this as a written task, audio visual recording is offered. The material prepared is then reviewed with the therapist. The harming father is asked to self-evaluate his prepared account using standards he has nominated or agreed to apply. This includes checking for:

- Clear messages of responsibility for his own actions.
- 'I said' and 'I did' descriptions, rather than 'we', which implies mutuality.
- Absence of interpretation and meaning, particularly interpretations suggesting the child co-participated in the behaviour or was motivated to do so.
- Clarity about time, place, frequency.
- How he acted to prevent disclosure or discovery of the sexual abuse.
- Forethought and planning.
- The ways he presented the sexual abuse of the child to others, including the mother.
- An absence of description of his feelings about the sexual abuse and other invitations to be focussed on his responses.

Once an initial account has been finalized, it is offered to his partner, who is not compelled to accept it. If she wishes to accept it, the way in which this occurs is negotiated on her terms with the support of her therapist.

In the meantime work with the mother can focus on her current understanding of, and questions she may be formulating about, the abuse and talking with her about day-to-day life as explored in Chapter 4. Almost invariably she

# 104 Conjoint work

is also managing the home and children by herself. It is not assumed the mother will or should agree to engaging in dyad work or receiving an acknowledgement by the harming father. However, once mothers become aware that their partners are preparing an acknowledgement they are usually interested to hear about this. This can build depth, authenticity and visibility of the harming father in his process. It also avoids misperceptions of the harming father being able to do this easily, or that what he is presenting has been 'sanitized' by the therapist and avoids the perception that the acknowledgement has been a joint effort by her partner and his therapist.

If the mother wishes to receive information from the harming father the process is by her design. How the acknowledgement will be received is not a negotiation between the parents as they are not in equal positions and the harming father is likely to attempt to control the process and specifically the mother's response and processing. The mother may choose to receive something in writing, seeing or hearing a recording or meeting in person. We learnt that in every instance of meeting in person, in addition to individual preparation, a written or recorded outline of acknowledgement, which the mother could receive and review with her therapist before meeting with the harming father, was essential. A video recording can be too intense if the harming father is speaking directly to camera. If this is the case an acknowledgment could take the form of a recorded interview of the harming father with his therapist, which the mother could later view together with her therapist. This minimizes the interpersonal transaction which can divert attention from the information being provided. It also provides the mother with an opportunity to respond in private first and then decide which aspects of her reaction she is prepared to share with the harming partner.

It is common in initial acknowledgements for the harming father to distance himself from agency for his own actions, offering descriptions such as: 'It happened on the days you were late coming home from work', rather than: 'I sexually abused our daughter on the evenings I knew you were at work'. The latter version is clearer about agency and removes an incorrect suggestion – unlikely to be missed by a mother – that but for being late coming home, she could have prevented the sexual abuse. Highlighting the differences between the versions is important as his initial attempts are highly likely to reflect a dominant narrative the harming father has held, shared with others and which may still be influential. It is also common for initial acknowledgments to contain invitations for the mother (or others) to be focussed on the parent who has abused in ways that divert attention from the child who was sexually abused. Preambles such as:

> I now realise how devastating my actions have been for you and the family. Dealing with this has been really hard for me and brought up memories of the abuse I suffered when I was a boy. I can't bear to think about what I have done and what I have lost.

Apart from the focus on self this description is typical in that it suggests beliefs about what may have caused him to sexually abuse.

Where a face-to-face meeting is the preferred process, both arrive separately. Ideally the building design provides separate entrances, waiting areas and therapy spaces. At Cedar Cottage the mothers generally preferred to be given the written 'face-up' to read either alone or with their therapist, to process her reactions briefly with her therapist and then meet with her partner/ex-partner. The woman chooses how this meeting proceeds. This may be to ask him to speak to his acknowledgement; to focus on how his account has changed since disclosure (which it usually has); ask clarifying questions; provide her response or a combination of these.

Preparation for both mother and the harming father includes agreement about taking breaks if needed and about how to end the meeting. Standards for conduct in the meeting were part of the preparation, most specifically for the harming father. These standards included: being respectful, safety in the room, listening, responding to questions and not becoming argumentative. Part of the harming father's preparation included becoming alert to the potential of becoming overwhelmed with a strong emotional response when facing the mother, his partner. He is invited to take a position against crying in order to avoid eliciting a care-based response from his partner, which distracts from the information contained in the face-up. This aspect of preparation aims to limit the effect of his inviting sympathy as an interpersonal tactic. If he does cry and invite sympathy, this can be processed through a lens of self-interest rather than sadness about the harm he has inflicted on everyone in the family.

In instances where mothers do not want any contact or interaction with the harming father, the written and/or recorded material can be made available to the mothers after being accepted on their behalf by their therapist. Unless the mother indicates otherwise, feedback is not provided to the harming father, including whether or not it has been accepted or how it has been received. Enquiries about this by the harming fathers inevitably address their own relational interests and a desire to manage the processes of others.

While the core purpose of an initial face-up to a mother is to provide information to support her belief, understanding and care for the child, it operates on many levels and also facilitates a number of other processes for her. Importantly it also provides an early opportunity for the harming father to take a position demonstrating his commitment to being 100 per cent responsible for his actions. The process of facing up as described here also means taking a position of being accountable and standing aside from the tactics used in sexually abusing the child and in self-protection, both during the abuse and following discovery. The appeal to do this is premised on an understanding that harming fathers can do so and should be motivated by seeking to do whatever they can to assist the recovery of people they have harmed. This commitment is tested when it comes at a perceived cost to self, usually loss of relationship(s), status and power.

## 106 Conjoint work

After initial face-up meetings parent dyad work typically focusses on practical issues of the mother's continuing care of the child(ren). Further parent dyad relational work does not proceed until the mother–daughter dyad has progressed as well as the mother–child's siblings dyad. The order of dyad work and timing is undertaken in close negotiation with the mother to respect her position as primary carer of the children. After a detailed face-up the harming father is encouraged to engage fully with his own therapy and demonstrate his commitment to the recovery of others by so doing. This is also evidenced by abiding by the conditions or standards to which he has committed. In relation to the family, the relevant standards are about not intruding on the physical and relational space of others.

### Mother–daughter

Mother–daughter work is less structured than parent dyad work and needs careful ongoing assessment due to the tactics to which both have been subjected by the father. The effect of the 'dominant story' of their relationship, orchestrated by the father's tactics, may not immediately be visible or accessible to them, especially where this has promoted a high level of interpersonal conflict. One matter to consider from the outset is that the child usually continues to live with her mother and siblings while the parent who abused is removed from the home. Mother and daughter are therefore communicating on a daily basis and the issue in relation to conjoint work is not so much when to do so but how to get on with day-to-day life and how to create safety for select, focussed discussions. Initially mothers may have many questions for their daughters.

> How did this all start? Was I ever nearby? Why did she not tell me? Why did she seem happy with him? Or prepared to go places with him?

Asking these questions may exacerbate tensions, be misunderstood as blaming the daughter and place an extra burden on the daughter to explain herself when she may be unable to. Rather, the mother can be advised to direct questions such as these to the harming father. Table 7.1 demonstrates how the mother's

*Table 7.1* Redirecting the mother's questions

| The mother's questions for daughter | Asking the harming father |
| --- | --- |
| How did this all start? | What did you do to start sexually abusing our daughter? |
| Was I ever nearby? | Where was I when you did this? Was I ever nearby? |
| Why did she not tell me? | How did you silence her? |
| Why did she go places with him? | How did you get her to go places with you and be alone? |

therapist can work with her to reframe the many questions that plague her in ways that both direct them to the father and place responsibility on him.

This approach avoids risking further harming the mother–daughter relationship and the responses from the harming father can affirm the mother's belief and understanding of her daughter. In effect this is preparation for the mother to join with her daughter. As described in Chapter 5, recognition by the mother of the daughter's experiences of harm and recognition of how each was subject to the tactics of the harming father are goals for this dyad. Both mother and daughter benefit from separate preparation for their joint counselling.

Secrecy, division and boundary violations are core tactics in parent–child sexual abuse. Recovery is best supported by openness and direct communication. Mothers frequently need support to access close adult friend or family support rather than to rely on any of their children. Making this explicit and setting up open communication are important steps. It is also helpful for the children to see their mother taking the lead in the organization of family life.

### Mother – daughter – siblings

Initially this is best managed as 'family meetings' with a business-like agenda, addressing topics such as arrangements for counselling, extra support extended family may be providing and new routines for the family. The initial aim is to establish this as the family unit. It is essential to acknowledge the harming father's absence and that he has harmed a child in the family. Siblings' questions about whether there is a future for the harming father with the family should be anticipated and planned for in therapeutic work with mothers and the victimized child, and, if possible, in their conjoint work. In the face of much uncertainty, therapists can work with the mother to navigate this complex situation in which her children may well have competing wishes and help her to avoid making any long term commitments as these may unduly influence or restrain recovery. A possible early response to plan with the mother is: 'It's too early; there's lots for us all to do and think about first.' However, even this type of response can be a source of anxiety for the victimized daughter if she has not had the opportunity in her own or her joint therapy with her mother to anticipate this reaction and her responses to it. This example speaks to the importance of integrating treatment and the therapeutic team carefully considering the timing of, and preparation for, conjoint work.

### Harming father – siblings

The mother needs to be present for direct work with siblings and the harming father. The daughter also needs to be aware that this is proposed and reassured about content and process. She may have strong views about what she does not want discussed, for example, not wanting any information about her to be passed on to the harming father. She may not want the details of what he did

# 108 Conjoint work

to her discussed by him with her siblings. These are both extremely important issues which need to be addressed in order to protect her integrity and privacy. For this reason, preparation of harming father and sibling work needs to include all family members.

Younger siblings may have difficulty understanding the significance of the sexual abuse. They may have experienced the harming father as positive and be grieving his absence and not being able to spend time with him. It is not unusual for the victimized daughter to advocate for younger siblings being able to have contact with the harming father in circumstances where she assesses her siblings not to be at risk of harm themselves and where she does not want to feel responsible for her siblings' unhappiness and grief. This occurs most commonly where younger siblings are boys and products of a relationship between the daughter's step-father and her mother. One consequence of harming father and sibling work in this context is a rapid progression of 'family expectation' that the harming father, mother and siblings can spend time together. This excludes the daughter from the family and should be avoided. The harming father and siblings' relationships should not be privileged over the siblings' relationships overall.

Early work for harming fathers and siblings is best focussed on communication to the siblings in age-appropriate ways, of what he has done and that this is the reason he is not with them. It can include acknowledgement of what he has committed to in his own counselling and outline his standards for supporting recovery of others, including non-intrusion. Siblings may be supported to ask the harming father questions either in person if they are meeting, or by letter if communicated by third parties, such as mother and counsellor. An example of an exchange in such an interview is:

FATHER: (to abused child's three siblings and mother): 'I'm not living at home with you because I hurt Annie (16 years). I did rude things to her and touched her private parts. I shouldn't have done that. I made her not tell about it and she didn't like it.'

SIBLING: (6 years, the youngest): 'Where are you living?'

FATHER: (to Counsellor): 'Am I allowed to say?'

COUNSELLOR: 'Not the address, but what district is it and what kind of place is it? Are you living alone?'

FATHER: (to children):'I am living close to where I work but that is a long way from where you live and go to school. I have a room with a bathroom in a house where men live and then go to work each day.'

SIBLING: (6 years): 'Why did you hurt Annie?'

FATHER: 'I don't know.'

SIBLING: (6 years): 'Are you going to find out?'

FATHER: 'I am trying to work that out with my counsellor.'

SIBLING: (6 years): 'When you find out are you going to tell us?'

FATHER: 'Yes' (appears uncomfortable and looks to the mother).

MOTHER: 'So while this is all happening we won't be seeing Dad for a while. I will be seeing him every now and then. What we all have to do is look after Annie and each other.'
SIBLING: (11 year old boy with developmental delay): 'I will look after Annie'. (Tears in his eyes, looking at father.)

In this case, each of the children was aware of Annie's sexual abuse by their father before the meeting. The purpose of the meeting was for the father to be clear about being responsible for harming Annie. The questions by the youngest child included a need to place his father in terms of where he was living. However, his question to his father about why he harmed Annie had not been anticipated by anyone. The father's look to the mother was a request to be rescued and supported. She did neither but attended to this most relevant issue for the children and herself. The 11 year old boy had been missing his father. The understanding he conveyed in the moment was also unexpected and profound.

### Harming father–daughter

As discussed, early direct contact between the harming father and victimized child is discouraged. It is important to find out about whether there has been or is currently any direct contact between them post disclosure. This involves more than checking that any child protection orders have been breached. Our experience is that harming fathers have difficulty remaining away and are eager to seek information about the child they harmed, in particular what the child is saying about them. Contact or information is often sought through family members, other third parties and social media. This intrusiveness can be expressed through offering advice to the mother on how to manage the child including 'support' to not 'put up with' behaviour which may include strong expressions of anger. All intrusions need to be stopped and the harming father helped to set a standard of not intruding in these and any other ways.

Contact for the daughter and harming father should only take place when she wants this, has undertaken preparation and is ready, is fully supported by her mother and it is in her best interests. Safety is the key consideration and the purpose of any contact needs to be addressed explicitly.

The victimized child will have received through third parties such as her therapist and mother information about the standards her father has set for himself and what he is saying about his sexual abuse of her. The harming father may suggest that contact by him may be helpful for his daughter but it is important that he does not perpetuate control of her by dictating the content or timing of her counselling. He may provide a face-up for her in counselling (via letter or recording), similar to what he provided for the mother. Unlike the mother, the daughter does not need validation of what he did to her to be able to believe. An example of a harming father-initiated contact is this letter.

## 110 Conjoint work

> Dear Jenny,
>
> I have been trying to write this letter for three days now, nothing that I write can make the pain I have caused you go away. I hope and pray that one day you maybe can find it in your heart to forgive me and maybe you can never be able to.
>
> I am proud of you for standing up for your rights. You were always my favourite one even though you were a bit of a devil. I love you kids more than life itself. Make everyone that loves you proud of you and forget about me so that you can go through life with a clear conscience.
>
> With all my heart. Please believe I love you forever.
>
> Dad

The letter was not sent and provides a good example of the need to prevent early direct communication. Jenny and her sister had been sexually abused by their father. Jenny was his favourite and her sister was deprived of contact with him except for 'special attention' when he sexually abused her. He only volunteered a letter for Jenny. The letter was useful for reviewing with the father in his therapy as it displayed several of his tactics and beliefs. It carries the hallmarks of a self-focussed communication and several layers of suggested co-responsibility. Jenny's mother and counsellor were informed that the letter had been delivered to the treatment program for Jenny. Later in the therapeutic process they asked for the letter so Jenny, her mother and sister could read and discuss it as part of their commitment to having a shared understanding of the harming father's tactics.

If the harming father provides a face-up for the victimized child it is accepted by the therapist. It is not necessarily presented to the child. In the first instance its contents are reviewed to ensure it is unlikely to cause harm should it be made available. This determination is made by the therapeutic team. It is not provided to the victimized child unless it is regarded as being helpful for her, the timing is right for her and her mother (who will have had opportunity to review it) is in full support. Issues to be aware of include: preventing re-traumatization or the harming father intruding in content or timing of the victimized child's recovery, ensuring any communication maintains the harming father as fully responsible and that a transactional process is not opened which re-establishes the past harming father–child dynamic. The harming father is not advised if the victimized child has been offered or accepted material he prepared or details of her reaction unless she explicitly wishes this to happen. Many harming fathers struggle with this as they believe they are entitled to know how the material they volunteer has been received. Not receiving this feedback is appropriate to the integrity of the victimized child and provides an opportunity for the harming father to address aspects of what he sees as his entitlement.

In the two year Cedar Cottage Program, if a face-up to the victimized child was not volunteered by the harming father at any stage, he was required as part of his participation in the program to do so by 16 months at the latest. If not anticipated by the victimized child or not fitting with her needs, it is stored indefinitely for her to access if she wishes at any time in the future, together with a program evaluation of it. At the conclusion of the harming father's participation in the program written confirmation is provided for the victimized child, her siblings and the mother. This includes confirmation of ongoing access to therapeutic services and that face-up material is held and can be made available, always with therapist support. A number of victimized children, as adults, recontacted Cedar Cottage in their own right to access this material and revisit aspects of their experience. Generally this was precipitated by life events such as: moving from home and becoming independent, wishing to review aspects of their relationship with their mothers, starting a family or after the death of the harming father.

If at any time the victimized child had questions for the harming father, these would be discussed with her therapist and mother. They would then be conveyed to the harming father and he was expected to respond. Questions asked included:

'What did you tell mum about me?'
'You said you loved me but you hurt me. Did you really love me? If you did love me what were you thinking when you abused me?'
'Why did you abuse me?'
'If I had not told, would you have kept going? If you stopped abusing me would you have started with (sister)?'

It is essential that harming father–victimized child dyad work does not isolate the child. Ideally the mother should be consulted and present throughout. If the mother is not available; physically, emotionally and psychologically, a decision needs to be made about whether to proceed.

> Rachel wished to see her father and had prepared for this with her therapist. Her mother Ann had also prepared as had Roy, Rachel's father. On the day this was to take place Rachel and Ann met with Rachel's therapist ahead of the scheduled meeting with Roy. Rachel appeared anxious and a little agitated. Ann was sullen and quiet. As they sat Ann knitted furiously and had no eye contact with Rachel. The therapist was not able to get clarity about the reasons for Rachel and Ann's presentation. While it could be possible this anxiety would abate once a meeting with Roy got underway, the therapist decided to call off the meeting as Rachel's safety was the primary consideration. Rachel and Ann were relieved when this decision was made and Roy was advised the therapy team called off the meeting as they decided the family was not ready. That is, the therapist took responsibility for the decision to call off the meeting.

## Conclusion

Similar processes apply to other dyad or relational combinations. This includes work with extended family members. Wherever possible permission is sought from those involved for the mother and daughter to be aware of who is joining the treatment efforts. Thorough preparation of all participants is essential and the therapeutic team needs to discuss and review the timing and progress of conjoint work and critically evaluate decisions about intervention against the principles underpinning the approach, as outlined in Chapter 2.

Through the process of revealing how he set up and maintained the abuse, isolated the victimized children and divided relationships, the harming father can take responsibility for his behaviour and contribute to essential steps to rebuild the damaged relationships. Importantly these include fundamental and longstanding sources of support for victimized children forging their long term safety.

## References

Jenkins, A. (1990). *Invitations to Responsibility: The Therapeutic Engagement of Men who are Violent and Abusive*. Adelaide, South Australia: Dulwich Centre Publications.

Sheinberg, M., & Fraenkel, P. (2001). *The Relational Trauma of Incest: A Family-based Approach to Treatment*. New York, NY: The Guilford Press.

# Chapter 8

# Work with the extended family

## Introduction

Pivotal to this approach and to forging enduring safety with parents who sexually assault their children is work with the extended family. Typically neglected in therapy, the family of the harming father are critical in three respects: as a means for creating safety from re-offending by the harming father; as individuals harmed by his actions; and as a source of support for the harmed child and her siblings. Work with the harming father's own family can also involve identifying and addressing other instances of abuse which may have never previously come to light.

In cases where the abuser is a step-father, the child's biological father is also affected. As a resource, a person who has experienced hurt and as a parent with a significant developmental relationship with his child, his needs also warrant attention. A central dimension of this work is that these relationships are all typically enduring, providing long term benefits for the child if they are effectively supported (or further losses if they are ignored).

## Work with the extended family

### Loss of the extended family

Children harmed by their parent, along with their siblings experience multiple and repeating losses which amongst others, typically include: stable family life, rights to develop their sexual identity without intrusion, a safe parental relationship and financial security. One loss that is often not appreciated by therapists is loss of the extended family, that is, loss of contact and support from the harming father's own family. Although not automatically the case, it is typical that the harming father's own family, in particular his parents, if they are still alive, will support him as part of enduring parental loyalty to their child, if for no other reasons. Shock, denial, shame, fear and the harming father's own minimization or tactics supply other reasons for this support.

A backdrop to the importance of this work is the body of research which establishes that the reactions of those close to the child are crucial to the impact

# 114 Work with the extended family

it has on the child (Herman, 1992). A second dimension to this is that there is a significant relationship between the supportiveness of those close to the child and the proximity of the abuser's relationship to the child, that is, the more distant the relationship, the more likely the child is to be supported and believed. In Diana Russell's (1986) research, girls who experienced incest and disclosed received supportive responses in only 31 per cent of cases where fathers and brothers were the abuser, increasing to 40 per cent and 65 per cent respectively with grandfathers and uncles as the perpetrator.

> Ken and Beverley were shattered by the police arrest of their son Tony (42) for the sexual abuse of his eight year-old daughter Tina. They have chosen to stand by Tony, who moved in with them after he was accepted into treatment and had to move out of the family home to comply with treatment conditions. Ken and Beverley are not very mobile. They want to maintain contact with their grandchildren, who include Tina's two younger brothers, aged six and four. They accept on face value that 'Tony did the wrong thing' but have not wanted to know more, accepting Tony's account that it was a one-off event, precipitated by a period of intense work-related stress. They have not spoken to the children's mother about Tony's assaults. As a result, the grandchildren are unable to see their grandparents. Tony's only sister, Nic (39) lives in a city which is four hours away by plane and has not had regular contact with her family for many years.

Through the actions of the harming father, his children risk exclusion from contact with the full extended family; this may include cousins, aunts and uncles and missing out on family gatherings such as Christmas. Due to issues of shame or blame, it is not uncommon for the extended family on the mother's side to be distant, which can exacerbate the social isolation the children experience.

## Work with grandparents

Grandparents are uniquely placed in children's lives to provide long term unconditional support and love, in general without the burden of daily parenting. The influence of grandparents is expanding, both in fact, through growing life expectancy, increasing rates of single parent families and grandparent carers, as well as in recognition of the roles they play as role models, encouragers, advisors, enforcers of norms and providers of emotional support (Dunifon, 2013). The stigma and isolation which parental incest brings to children, make this support, by those who know 'the secret', even more critical.

In order to offer this support in a meaningful way, the harming father needs to provide a detailed face-up to his own parents. This face-up needs to be delivered early in treatment by the harming father himself in the therapy setting with his parents, describing his tactics to establish and maintain the abuse, as well as the duration, frequency and intrusiveness of offences. The face-up, as with conjoint work with other close family members, documented in Chapter 7, also needs to articulate any tactics the harming father has used to portray the mother or victimized child as culpable, complicit or not credible. The face-up from their son frees up the grandparents to express belief and potentially remorse to the harmed child and resume a supportive relationship with their grandchildren. This material makes it very difficult for the harming father to maintain a victim-stance, which may have been the case before a face-up occurs.

Grandparents need time to absorb and process this potentially shattering new view of their son. If contact is to resume with their grandchildren, a process needs to be initiated in which the children's mother is consulted and consents to this. The grandparents need support to consider how to respond to the victimized child: establishing what they may need to say and do to indicate their support. Attention is paid to the abused child's right to privacy, so that the grandparents do not become conduits of photographs and news about the victimized child, which the harming father may use for his own purposes. In most instances it is unhelpful to have an adult son move back in with parents, who are often frail and can come to rely on their son, which may heighten their vulnerability to his influence. For this reason therapists should exclude this as a safe accommodation option for the harming father, other than in exceptional circumstances.

## Inter-generational harm

The harming father's family may include people who have abused the harming father during his childhood. If a now adult sibling or a parent is responsible for abuse of the harming father in his childhood, this is a factor to consider both in relation to ability for that person to support the family and for the harming father to resolve issues of his own victimization. The nature of any historic harm and its current meaning, including the degree to which it has been recognized and resolved, needs to be understood and assessed as part of any work with extended family. It can be regarded as a matter of fairness that a harming father should also expect restitution for historic harm he has suffered. There is no need to prioritize work on his harm ahead of work for the recovery of the victimized child. Both can be managed at the same time. He is not guaranteed the person who harmed him will be available to a joint process. However working on this may be helpful for him to take responsibility for his sexually abusive behaviour, including his development of a responsible explanation which incorporates his own abuse experiences.

## Bringing others in on the story

While the harming father's own parents and family can play a crucial role in supporting the victimized child and siblings, they are also the individuals who are most

## 116   Work with the extended family

likely to maintain ongoing contact with the harming father throughout his life. In this regard, they are an essential key to holding him accountable and reducing future re-offence and are therefore an important focus for therapeutic intervention.

In this approach we employ the concept of 'audience' that is, the creation of an ongoing group of individuals who are aware of the actions of the harming father, his risk factors for re-offence and his strategies for avoiding this. Further explored in Chapter 9, the therapeutic work starts with issuing a written introduction and invitation to the harming father's own parents and other close family members. By taking charge of this process and actively leading with information, the therapist or agency can ensure family members are provided with accurate information about his therapy and offences, as well as initiate support for them. A typical letter to family members introduces the therapist, the agency and its aims, making it clear that there is no 'cure' for the behaviour, which involves secrecy and avoidance of responsibility. It then introduces the idea of an audience to the harming father's behaviour, that is, a group of significant people in his life who are aware of his history, and the goals and standards he is setting to lead a life free from abuse. Working pro-actively, the therapist notifies the letter recipient of the time and date they will make contact to follow up the letter. The full text of a sample letter used at Cedar Cottage for potential audience members is included below.

> Audience Sample Letter
> Dear ...............
>
> I am a Treatment Co-ordinator at Cedar Cottage and am writing to you concerning (harming father's name (H)). H has informed me that you are aware of his participation in the program and that you are agreeable to have contact with Cedar Cottage. I understand from H that you are aware that the reason for his participation relates to his abusive conduct towards his (daughter/son) over a period of time.
>
> Cedar Cottage is a place that helps families where one or more of the children have been sexually abused by a parent or step-parent. Help is offered to every member of the family, as we believe each may have been affected in some way by the abuse. A variety of services are offered so as to best meet the different needs of each family member. These services, funded by the NSW Department of Health, are provided free of charge.
>
> There are two main aims of the program at Cedar Cottage:
>
> - Firstly, that the victims and their family feel safe and are supported in their recovery.
> - Secondly, to assist persons who have sexually assaulted children from sexually abusing again. The parent who has abused must acknowledge full responsibility for the abuse and work towards attending to the harm he has caused to the family. Therapy assists him to see the harmful nature of his actions and to be aware of the impact of his sexual abuse on the family.

Our work with H and other men who have conducted themselves in similar ways indicates that there is no 'cure' for this conduct. It is a matter of H needing to remain alert to the risk of re-offending and of returning to abusive and disrespectful ways of relating to others. H's abusive actions involved secrecy and avoidance of responsibility. Making himself accountable to significant people in his life is an essential component of his treatment. To develop personal responsibility and accountability, H will need to have significant people in his life who are aware of his history, and of the goals and standards he sets to lead a life free from abuse. We call this group of persons an 'audience'. H has nominated you as a potential member of his audience. The significant issues for audience members, as we see it, are that they are aware of H's history and his participation in treatment and have sufficient ongoing contact with him to be in a position to evaluate:

- his progress towards his treatment goals,
- his conduct, and
- the changes he is making in himself.

Being a member of H's audience does not make you responsible for his actions, nor are you responsible for whether or not he re-offends. Being a member of his audience, however, does require you to keep up to date with H's treatment and to be willing to give him clear and honest feedback. I have enclosed an information package. I would like to call you on dd/mm/yy to arrange a time to further discuss any matters or questions you may have about H's participation in the program and the role of an audience member. I look forward to speaking with you.

Yours faithfully

Treatment Coordinator

The correspondence is sent after the harming father has first spoken to the family member or other potentially suitable member of their audience and gained their consent to receive a letter. It is not unusual for a harming father to – at least initially – oppose this development in therapy. In such instances he is given the opportunity to explain why he believes it is inappropriate for his parents or close family members to be involved in this way. The child's mother is also given a chance to veto choice of 'audience members' if she believes they represent unsafe options who will collude with offending behaviour.

In some cases, immediate family members may be too burdened by dealing with the personal impact of the abuse, to take on the role of audience, so other significant persons in the harming father's life, such as an employer, family friend or cousin are also invited to play this role.

## Harming father's siblings as earlier victims

In line with the evidence that sexually abusive behaviour often commences early in life (Fulu et al., 2013), one in five of the men treated at Cedar Cottage

## 118 Work with the extended family

had started sexually abusing as juveniles (Goodman-Delahunty, 2014). Of the men who disclosed sexually abusive behaviour prior to adulthood, all had harmed close family members, typically sisters or cousins. On most occasions these assaults had gone unreported and undetected, which had significant implications for engaging the harming father's family members.

### Ethics and practice of approaching former victims

In some instances the adult siblings may disclose their experiences of childhood abuse by the harming father in the context of therapy. More commonly, we became aware of these events through the harming father's disclosures in the course of assessment or treatment with 55 per cent of the men who entered treatment reporting prior offences (Goodman-Delahunty, 2014).

This situation confronts therapists with the ethical dilemma of what should be done in response to these disclosures, whether the previous victims should be contacted and offered support and further reports to police should be made. An adult who has not made a disclosure or sought assistance for abuse they have experienced has rights to privacy and to making choices about sharing this information. Action on an unsolicited disclosure by the harming father of his earlier abusive acts, denies her this choice. Over some years of practice and wrestling with this dilemma, it was determined that the most ethically sound practice involved the police making contact with previous victims, where this was possible. The man was required to visit a police station and make a statement; police would then approach the victimized person. It was essential that no victimized person felt pressure to participate in a program or to contribute to the harming father's therapy. This approach is consistent with the harming father taking a stance of responsibility for his actions, including dealing with the consequences of additional police investigations and potentially court proceedings.

The women were then offered the opportunity to meet with program therapists, on the basis that this would be purely for their own benefit. The choice to attend an alternative therapist or service, was an option also offered to the women. Where women elected to meet with the therapist, the focus was on exploring her reaction to the disclosure, needs and questions arising from this and restoring her sense of control. In some instances this may involve receiving a face-up from the harming father, if this is wanted.

Nic accepted an offer from her brother Tony's therapist to fly in and have a meeting. In the course of his therapy, Tony had disclosed how he had introduced Nic to the 'shed game' when he was aged 15 and she was 12. This game started as mutual, showing each other their genitals, itself age inappropriate, but over time it progressed to full penetration. Tony threatened Nic that if she told their parents he would expose her at school as a 'slut', which had effectively silenced her. Nic decided that she did not want to meet with Tony or receive any information from him, but over three meetings with the therapist processed her own experiences. Following this she offered to write a short statement about her experiences and the impact it had on her, on the understanding that this would be provided to her parents, and if deemed useful, to her niece Katie who had also been abused by Tony. Ken and Beverley were deeply saddened when they were invited in to read and discuss Nic's statement. Over time, however, they began to understand her emotional and physical distancing of herself from the family and reached out to express their support and sorrow.

All the women who were contacted in this way expressed relief and gratitude at the opportunity to discuss their experiences; in particular they valued finding out that the abuser was finally being held to account for his actions.

## Non-harming fathers

Harming parents are more likely to be step-fathers than biological fathers. In most of these cases, the child's biological father is still a part of his children's life and has complex reactions of his own, which can often impact negatively on the mother and child/ren. Alternatively, the mother may have a new partner, with the biological father being the abuser. Either way, the non-harming father can play a key role in contributing to positive outcomes for the child and family. This is particularly the case when the offender is the biological father and the non-harming father has an ongoing relationship with the child's mother and the siblings.

### Issues of anger, guilt, and prior abuse

A common reaction on the part of non-harming fathers is intense anger at the harming father and/or the mother, who is often seen to be equally or more culpable for choosing an unsafe partner and not keeping the child safe. In general, non-harming fathers do not have primary care or custody of the children, which can heighten their sense of being disenfranchised and lacking opportunities to influence the situation.

Feelings of guilt are also common, for not 'being there' to protect the child. Dominant discourses of mother blame and of children as property feed into these reactions on the part of non-harming fathers, meaning that self-righteous indignation is a predictable initial and sometimes sustained response. Issues of anger and guilt need to be addressed with the non-harming father to provide a supportive environment for the victimized child and mother to heal. An individual therapy session with the father can provide the opportunity to express and

120    Work with the extended family

explore these reactions and consider, from the child's perspective, what would be most helpful for her to hear and experience from him.

Sometimes the relationship with a father has been marked by its own violence or abuse. Women who have previously experienced abusive relationships are sometimes targeted by men who are interested in sexually abusing children, who employ tactics designed to lead them to be appreciative and protective towards them for treating them in ways that represent a singular improvement in comparison to an earlier partner. This situation can compound women's struggle to believe that their new partner has sexually abused their child, because he is 'so much better than the last one'. These men represent a minority of those who sexually abuse children, however the results for the mothers, when this occurs, are often devastating.

Mothers who have experienced earlier domestic violence, can also experience compounded self-blame or self-doubt, and be persuaded to the view that there is something intrinsic to their personality that attracts abusive men. This is often expressed as 'feeling that there is a target painted on my forehead'. Intervention with mothers and children can address these beliefs, in the same way that intervention with non-harming fathers who have been abusive can be used to identify opportunities to make redress for former harms done.

### Intervention for safety

Safety for the victimized child is established through inviting the non-harming father to set standards for himself in relation to his behaviour towards his children. When anger has been expressed by a father, a useful conversation is one in which he is invited to consider the impact of his threats to hurt the harming parent or anger towards the mother and whether this brings him closer to his children. Inviting him to consider what he could do to be safe and supportive for his children, whilst acknowledging his range of reactions, can assist him to make an important contribution to his children's recovery.

The work of addressing parental sexual assault, as this chapter has outlined, is clearly not limited to the harming father, the child or even the immediate family members, but importantly includes the extended family, particularly the non-harming father who has a clear role to play in supporting children's recovery, mother's relief from blame, accountability of harming parents and forging enduring safety.

## References

Dunifon, R. (2013). The influence of grandparents on the lives of children and adolescents. *Child Development Perspectives*, 7(1), 55–60.

Fulu, E., Warner, X., Miedema, S., Jewkes, R., Roselli, T., & Lang, J. (2013). *Why Do Some Men Use Violence against Women and Can we Prevent it? Quantitative Findings from* the UN Multi-country Study on Men and Violence in Asia and the Pacific. Retrieved from Bangkok: http://www.partners4prevention.org/sites/default/files/resources/p4p-report.pdf

Goodman-Delahunty, J. (2014). Profiling parental child sex abuse. *Trends & Issues in Crime and Criminal Justice*. Retrieved from http://www.aic.gov.au/media_library/p ublications/tandi_pdf/tandi465.pdf

Herman, J. L. (1992). *Trauma and Recovery*. USA: Basic Books.

Russell, D. (1986). *The Secret Trauma: Incest in the Lives of Girls and Women*. New York: Basic Books.

# Chapter 9

# Building safety

## Introduction

This chapter provides a description of how safety is considered and promoted from the outset of the program. As discussed earlier, the concept of safety for the victimized child is broad, encompassing not only physical but emotional and psychological safety, which requires validation of the full extent of harm suffered and restored relationships with her mother, siblings and other extended family members. While elements of the program will be familiar to the reader from Chapter 3, the focus of this chapter is on the ongoing work with the harming father to build safety.

## Building safety into the assessment

### Accountability

Accountability and visibility of the harming father is central to the safety and well-being of all family members. The invitation for harming fathers to engage in a therapeutic process is framed around these and related principles. In a parallel process the program demonstrated commitment to these same principles. Detailed written information about the program and expectations of participants was forwarded prior to the first assessment interview. This material included: a program *Ethos Statement* which outlines beliefs, principles and concepts of the program (Wyre, 1990), an orientation booklet for program participants containing a sample treatment agreement, legal rights and responsibilities, headline issues for therapy, review processes and core treatment activities.

The mother receives the same information and material tailored for her and the children. This follows the first assessment session of the harming father at which he is asked to consent to the mother being advised that he has asked for assessment. The assessment cannot go ahead without him consenting to this, which in turn leads to asking about the mother and children's wishes and services being offered to them. In most instances the mothers were aware of the harming father's request. Despite this process being in place as a program requirement, a number of harming fathers argued (unsuccessfully) for their participation in the program with no input or participation by the mother or family.

Scepticism that providing a large volume of written material results in the harming father merely reciting commitment to the content of these documents is dispelled as he is asked to provide a detailed account of his conduct and how he represented this to others at the time of the abuse, in the period after disclosure and currently. As entry to the Cedar Cottage Program required a conviction based on a plea of guilty, the assessment focussed from the outset on the requirement that the applicant acknowledge the full range of his harmful behaviours towards the victim and other family members. Even with this in place as a legislative framework, most applicants brought into the assessment minimizations and other types of denial as discussed in Chapter 3.

In the first assessment interview the applicant's responses to the *Ethos Statement* were sought. The most common response by the men was to agree with all the content and at times they expressed gratitude for having the content available and revelations made possible. This was noted but neither accepted nor processed in detail at the time. It is important to not engage in exchanges to review responses at this early stage before the framework for him to assess his own conduct has been established. The assessor needs to be alert to the likelihood that responses by the harming father at this stage will reflect patterned behaviour on his part intended to impress or otherwise influence the assessor.

### Goals, standards and plans of action

Definitions and examples of goals, standards and plans of action are included in the *Orientation Booklet* and are core concepts throughout treatment. Setting expectations for standards of behaviour is central to creating safety by assessing whether the harming father applies himself to these standards. Taking into account the program materials provided, the applicant is asked to outline his hopes and expectations. The structured first step in developing self-evaluation and self-awareness, which also includes recognition of others, is shaping the goals and setting standards by which he will measure his performance.

Initial goals put forward by harming fathers frequently include:

- To be trusted
- To return home and be a family again
- For everyone to get better (recover)
- To apologize and be forgiven

The concept of standards is less familiar initially and was at times limited to:

- To be fully honest

Starting with this standard, the idea of being 'fully honest' is tested by asking what being *less* than fully honest means or looks like. This highlights that anything less than complete honesty means dishonesty and/or deception, that is, dishonesty can be through omission.

The harming father's initial goals are reviewed in a number of ways including a check on which goals are for the applicant alone and which are for the benefit of others. It is also important for the therapist to check whether the harming father has missed goals for anybody harmed or affected by his actions. A single goal is selected for testing against principles in the *Ethos Statement* and first standards the harming father sets. An example of a goal is to 'apologize and be forgiven'. The therapist asks the man to be more specific. Apologize to whom? For what? This requires him to talk about his sexually abusive behaviours. Exploration of who knows what and how they know usually confirms that the harming father is relying on the child victim's description. He may or may not have spoken with other family members, most importantly the child's mother. By relying on the child's statement the harming father is choosing to measure his acknowledgement against what she has been able to say, which is consistent with research that disclosure is a measured and incomplete account structured around questions asked in a forensic interview (Esposito, 2015). The man is guided to review his goals and standards to set a goal of describing his sexual abuse of the child victim fully and in his own words. The purposes of this are multiple. Firstly he needs to satisfy the assessor that his acknowledgement of the sexual abuse is genuine and not strategic or instrumental. That is, his acknowledgement is not to avoid imprisonment while maintaining his control over the information that is shared with other family members. At the same time it is unrealistic to expect self-interest is not at play, as avoiding imprisonment was structured into this scheme as a legislated incentive for men to take responsibility for their actions. An overarching goal is for the harming father to demonstrate he accepts responsibility and in doing so set a standard that he does not leave the burden of telling with the child (Jenkins, 1990).

### Developing a complete account of the abuse

The task of describing his actions has the confronting title of *Crime Description*. The crime description is prepared during assessment and again at 8 and 16 months into treatment. The initial crime description has specific instructions for the harming father as a program applicant at that point in time. He is asked to not refer to the child's police statement (if he has access to it) and to avoid responding to the specific charges as these may be limited descriptions of sexual abuse he repeated over time. In the later repetition of this task the harming father is expected to provide greater recognition of his internal processes; incorporate more detail of his actions; demonstrate increased recognition of the impact of his actions; and generally be reflective of his progress in therapy.

Excerpt from Crime Description Task instruction.

The Crime Description task is for you to set out, in writing, your sexually abusive actions. There is an expectation on the Program's part that your Crime Description will be a growing one; unfolding and becoming more detailed and complete as you take further steps to own your actions, to re-attribute responsibility for your conduct to yourself, and become clearer about the differences between excuses and responsible explanations.

Your Crime Description should include:

- What you said and did in carrying out the assaults.
- Your beliefs, thoughts (things you said to yourself) and feelings at the time of the assaults.
- What you said and did during the planning of the abuse.
- What you said and did around the time of the disclosure.
- Your beliefs, thoughts and feelings during the planning and around the time of disclosure.
- The impact of your actions on others. That is, how the things you did and said have affected other individuals and their relationships. You should not limit yourself to thinking of the effects upon your direct victim(s) alone.

   There are many issues to be addressed in your Crime Description. Some of the questions you should attend to include:
- Has my account of what I said and did validated the statements made by my victims?
- How old was my victim when I first started assaulting?
- How old was my victim when I first began thinking about my victim sexually?
- Have I been clear about how often I sexually assaulted?
- If I moved from one type of abuse to another or changed the nature of the abuse over time, have I been clear about this?
- Have I clearly separated: (a) what I said and did (which my victim experienced) from (b) all the things that were going on inside me at the time (my thoughts, feelings and beliefs)?
- Have I left out any significant people or relationships impacted by my abuse?
- Have I described what my child victim(s) did and said? And how I responded to this?

The terminology used by the assessing therapist can be confronting for the applicant. Applicants are asked initially what they call their actions and to introduce notions such as how the men planned sexual abuse of their daughters and worked to avoid detection.

BRYCE: 'I just want her to be able to be OK, considering all that happened.'
THERAPIST: 'All that happened?'
BRYCE: 'Well, you know, with what happened and all ...'

## 126 Building safety

THERAPIST: 'Are you meaning what you did to Ebony?'

BRYCE: 'Yes?'

THERAPIST: 'And what do you call what you did to Ebony?'

BRYCE: 'You mean the sexual things?'

THERAPIST: 'You may know what other people might call what you did. But what do you call it when you think about it now?'

BRYCE: 'I guess it's sexual abuse but I didn't think about it that way.'

THERAPIST: 'How are you able to see it that way now?'

BRYCE: 'She didn't really have a say in it. I mean I didn't really give her a choice....'

THERAPIST: 'So being able to call this is sexual abuse means facing how you did this to Ebony. What is it taking for you to be able to do this?'

BRYCE: 'I do want the best for her. The book you sent me to read got me thinking about how I really wanted it to not be so bad, but when you make me put a name on it ... it's bad, it really is.'

THERAPIST: 'Seems naming your actions means also facing what you did in more detail. Do you think you can keep going with that?'

BRYCE: 'I'll have to ... I want to ... and hope I can.'

Bryce at this early stage struggles with minimization and avoidance but when direction is provided by the therapist he manages to name his behaviour as sexual abuse, albeit tentatively and he immediately goes to a richer description of how he did this. There is clearly more work for Bryce. The motivational questions and observations of the therapist are important to let Bryce know his efforts are being noticed and decrease the potential for Bryce to retreat from the steps forward he makes here. At times men have reconsidered naming their actions as sexual abuse, usually worried about rejection by family members. Here Bryce identifies he 'didn't really give her (Ebony) a choice'. This is a strong statement by Bryce as a starting point to taking responsibility. Bryce can be asked several questions about this:

How did you not give Ebony a choice? Was it significant for you to believe Ebony had a choice? Have you said or suggested to others Ebony had a choice?

Bryce's responses can provide detail about Bryce's actions in sexually abusing Ebony, his tactics in representing this to others and ultimately confirm how Ebony never had choice and was not responsible for his sexual abuse of her in any way.

Many harming parents arrive at assessment with a view their actions were unplanned, spontaneous and poorly judged expressions of affection and love. Disentangling this is significant for the man to clearly identify his own processes and choices. It is also important for the child's emotional and psychological safety to be believed and for her experience of the sexual abuse and relationship

Building safety 127

with her father to be understood, for all family members to see how they have been directly influenced by the father and how their relationships have been affected.

Before being given the crime description task, the harming father is asked to indicate who knows about his sexual abuse of the daughter, whom he has spoken with and what he has said. Listing who knows is often based on third person reports (mostly from the mother) and the men have generally not spoken with many people. Where they have spoken with the mother rarely have they spoken in any detail, but the detail of what they said is important to note and come back to as inevitably the initial responses fall far short of taking responsibility for their actions, contain minimizations and are heavily laden with explanations and a focus on themselves.

John indicated at his first assessment interview that he had taken full responsibility for sexually abusing his daughter Jacinta, and that he had spoken directly with his wife Jenny in doing so. When asked about this conversation it became clear he had taken a position of overall responsibility but relied on Jenny having spoken with Jacinta and the child protection workers and police about Jacinta's disclosure. Jenny believed Jacinta and from the outset took the position that John had to take responsibility for his actions. John had stressed to Jenny he never intended to hurt Jacinta and his evidence of this was that during his sexual abuse he checked if she was okay and told her she could tell him to stop. Sometimes she *had* told him to stop. He had not spoken with Jenny in detail about how and what he did and his account to her highlighted his feelings and beliefs rather than presenting a clear picture of his actions and therefore, Jacinta's experience. John also indicated in the assessment that Jacinta's account was accurate with the exception of one incident which he said 'did not happen'. He said he planned to plead guilty to this as to do otherwise would be worse for Jacinta and the family. John had not spoken with Jenny about this, had no definite plan to do so, but said he would if required and believed she would understand why he would do this.

Several of John's strategies are evident in this description. At this stage his degree of influence over Jenny is unknown. She was engaged in a parallel process during the assessment which was framed as an opportunity to gain a fuller picture of John's abusive behaviour, seek her advice and express any other requests she had. Programs need to be alert to the possibility of the harming fathers seeking to position their partners to believe that the men's prospects of coming into treatment were dependent upon how the women participated in the assessment.

This was John's first response to the program inviting him to provide a Crime Description, consistent with his commitment to taking full

128  Building safety

responsibility. A decision was made not to begin by addressing John's denial or how he was attempting to position Jenny. John struggled with the task. His first attempt was a mix of his feelings, beliefs and observations of others. Once he had separated his explanations and beliefs from a description of his actions the issue of his denial was able to be addressed. John was asked what his denial of the single incident suggested about Jacinta and how this measured up to his commitment to taking responsibility. He showed he understood this concerned Jacinta's reputation as he immediately said she 'would not lie' about this. Alternatives were then canvassed including whether he was suggesting she was an unreliable historian, if she had mental health issues which affected her disclosure and if so, were these connected to his sexual abuse of her. The assessor declined the invitation to collude with John pleading guilty while maintaining he had not committed this act. The assessor also avoided any consideration of Jacinta's motivations, choosing instead to focus on what this denial by John meant.

One expectation during assessment is that the applicant provides the mother with a clear description of his actions as discussed in detail in Chapter 7. For John it meant at the same time he was preparing and reviewing his crime description and related material, he would be making it available to Jenny. It was made clear to Jenny that she was under no obligation to accept any material or to meet with John. Jenny opted to meet with John in person and accepted a suggestion he prepare a written outline for her to receive prior to meeting.

John decided between assessment sessions that he would acknowledge that all Jacinta's disclosure was true. He indicated the part he denied was the most shameful aspect of his behaviour and he feared it could result in Jenny stopping all contact with him. Both of John's reasons indicate self-protection to the exclusion of others' well-being. At the same time, his decision was based on a level of recognition of the importance to Jacinta of her experiences being fully acknowledged.

Building enduring safety requires the harming father providing accurate information and so giving the opportunity for individuals to process what this means for themselves and others. Jenny's processing of John's information includes the detail in his crime description as well as his strategies in managing others, including her. Recognizing how he positioned and managed her is likely to challenge her perception of him, herself and her judgement about their relationship.

### Establishing an audience to change

As outlined in Chapter 8, developing an audience to change is another foundational safety strategy put into place during assessment. The early Narrative Therapy consideration of 'audience' is extended beyond the concept of 'outsider-witness' in which people may tell or perform their story to an 'audience' as a pivotal therapeutic experience (White, 2005), to engaging an audience of closely known people to witness over time how the person is living his life to standards he has made available to them. These include a core commitment to safety and respecting others around him.

An audience is a group of people who are significant in the life of the harming father and family, who are aware or can be made aware of the harming father's sexual abuse behaviour and are well-placed to support and evaluate changes made by the harming father. Selection of audience members involves the child's mother approving audience members and perhaps nominating who may be suitable. The child's privacy and other needs must also be taken into account. As the child's mother is also a direct victim of the harming father, it is not appropriate for her recovery to be an audience member.

The rationale for establishing an audience is that leaving all elements of safety to be managed within a family is risky, as the opportunity for the harming father to retain a position of privilege and power is greatest when visibility and accountability have narrowest focus. This becomes riskier still if management is based solely or predominantly on the harming father's self-report. Care needs to be taken that audience members support the harming father's efforts to take responsibility and are not vulnerable to excusing him or shifting responsibility or blame from him to others. They should also be available to the child's mother and program staff. Ideally audience members are drawn from different domains of harming father's life which include:

- Family – most commonly adult siblings or harming father's parents. This is a balancing act at times because this group are also grandparents, aunts, uncles, in-laws to the victimized child, her siblings and mother.
- Social – preferably long-term and close friends.
- Workplace – preferably employer or supervisor, rather than an employee or person who reports to him. Men usually need to negotiate regular time off work for therapy, making recruitment of audience from workplace less onerous than it first appears. Only one man in the program lost his employment due to disclosure to an employer. This was not as a result of seeking an audience member but due to the potential for unsupervised access to children in the course of his work.
- Religious affiliation – where the harming father is an active participant in a faith based group an invitation to a leader, usually Minister, Pastor, Priest or Rabbi, became standard and invitations tended to be actively accepted.

One positive aspect of audience development beyond its function as an immediate circle for accountability and feedback is that it breaks through isolation of parent–child sexual abuse as a 'family matter' and is recognition of the broader context of the harming parent and family's lives.

## 130   Building safety

### *Treatment agreement*

The conclusion of assessment is marked by the formalizing of a treatment agreement specifically tailored to the needs of the family. Over time the conditions became standard with an individually designated exclusion zone and other conditions. The agreement specifies limitations on where the harming father may live, travel, with whom he may have contact and includes consent to share information with named persons or authorities. The conditions were then presented to the Court, which finalized the diversion process and confirmed that the conditions were 'reasonable'. A summary of treatment conditions to commence participation typically included:

- Live independently and away from the family
- No contact with the victimized child or her siblings irrespective of age
- Not reside with or have contact with, except as incidental to day-to-day life, children under 16 years old
- Not visit the family home without express permission
- Not threaten or harass any family members
- To seek or maintain paid employment or training activity
- To register as a patient in a general medical practice and have a full assessment of physical health
- Consent for communication by the program with family and relevant agencies
- No contact with other program participants except during group therapy sessions

These conditions were developed from the program's experience in responding to harming fathers' behaviours, which were unsafe or which undermined therapy. These types of behaviours are exemplified by Mitch.

> Mitch had an AVO stating he should not come within 500 metres of the child he victimized or her place of residence or any person who resided with her. Mitch and his family lived in a regional centre with a population of just over 20,000. Mitch's daughter and one of her two her siblings frequently saw him or his car and both developed hypervigilance about seeing him and withdrew from a number of regular activities they would otherwise engage in.

Mitch's story was typical in that he disregarded the victimized child's fear and mixed views of the siblings about him.

Over time Cedar Cottage developed an expanded definition for harming fathers of 'no contact' with children, based on experience with different men in the program which demonstrated the importance of providing examples and emphasized seeking advice and permission and not acting on assumptions.

You cannot visit or have any other contact with any of the children in the family without the written permission of the Director. If any of the named children turn 16, this does not mean you can begin having contact (for this reason). Contact includes such things as:

- Driving by the house
- Talking through other people (e.g. 'tell the kids I said hello')
- Sending letters or cards
- Giving presents
- Talking on the phone or leaving messages
- Waving from a distance
- Attending the same church service
- 'Accidentally' speaking with a child when ringing to speak with your partner/ex-partner
- Sending e-mails to any member of the household where your victim/s live

This is not a complete list. Direct and indirect contact is not allowed. If you are in any doubt, do not act without contacting your therapist.

The 'no contact' with family requirement should not extend to the mothers unless they do not want to be contacted by the harming father. Mothers often required contact with the men to attend to the details of day-to-day life. However this contact was reviewed with the women as the 'need' for contact may be built upon beliefs or processes in which the harming father retains a position of substantial control and the mother finds it difficult to see she her ability to manage without him. The mothers did not have restrictions placed upon them but the men often tried to align with the mothers and against the program.

Greg rented an apartment after disclosure he had sexually abused his 15 year old step-daughter Trish. He rented the apartment across town from the family home but quite close to where Trish's mother Susan worked. Greg said he agreed with Susan that as she worked shifts it would be better for her to stay with him several nights a week. As Trish lived in the family home with her 16 year old sister who attended the same school, Greg and Susan felt this arrangement was fine. The program insisted that Greg have no person cohabiting with him as a number of therapeutic steps had stalled, notably Susan and Trish speaking about Greg's sexual abuse of Trish, which this arrangement would make more difficult. Greg was expected to take a position of promoting the recovery of others and not place himself between mother and victimized child. In this case he attempted to present this as Susan's idea and his interest and role in developing the plan was not initially clear. It is also a matter of concern regarding the safety of Trish and her sister, in terms of their being left alone in this way and at this time.

## 132    Building safety

The example of Greg above is of a clearly designed interruption of the family's recovery. There were other issues in relation to contact between parents which needed close review.

> Barry abided by all of his treatment conditions but was lonely. He spoke with his partner Connie and arranged they would have a system where he would call most nights after dinner, allowing the phone to ring twice and then hanging up. Connie could then decide based on what was happening at home whether to call back. She usually did and the conversations were hushed until she went outside. Sometimes they were long as well.

The children worked out quickly that it was Barry who was calling. When they talked about this with their counsellors, which was the first time the program became aware of this, they said they understood their mother wanted to speak with Barry but were not happy about this almost nightly intrusion. Reviewing this with Connie and Barry separately the program acknowledged the wishes of the adults to speak with each other. However this was a regular reminder to all of Barry's presence and occurred at a critical time for the family household, the end of the day as the children prepared for bed and school the next day. A new routine was encouraged for Connie to spend time with each of the two children every night. Barry was thereafter not allowed to call the family home under any circumstance, removing awareness and any anxiety that he may be on the phone. Connie and Barry made arrangements to speak during the day and were encouraged to limit this to every few days and review this in their individual therapy. They were not engaged in joint therapy until Connie and the children had made progress in their conjoint therapy.

The requirement for medical assessment was developed as the program noted the harming fathers in general had paid little attention to their physical health. Previously undiagnosed matters were identified as well as general lifestyle health related issues: obesity, blood pressure, heart related conditions. Concerns regarding mental health were able to be managed including referral for psychiatric assessment if indicated, which was usually for depression and in some instances was for management of psychosis or suicidality. A family safety-related issue arose in the cases where the men continued with pre-existing medical and dental arrangements; they ran the risk of encountering family members and on a number of occasions tried to speak with the family doctor or dentist about the victimized child or other family members.

The condition requiring no contact with other program participants outside of the program became a general condition after a number of incidents. These included the discovery that the men were meeting at a nearby coffee shop before group therapy sessions and discussing how to manage the group session. Other incidents of contact included one man offering another work at his place of employment, who then sought private 'coaching' from that man to be able to appear successful in therapy. The man offered the work was told the work would be withdrawn, possibly reported to the program if he did not agree to secretly help the first man. The extortion used was very similar to extortion the man demanding help had used in abusing his daughter.

Each of the treatment conditions were discussed with the mother as well as the harming father. Her advice was sought regarding every condition and frequently family members and mutual friends were identified as people the mother wished to maintain support from and to have clear conditions around the harming father's interactions with these people. In many instances the mothers were shocked at how the harming father would attempt to obtain updates on the family from sources without her knowledge.

A safety standard of the program was the return of men to Court for sentencing if they seriously breached treatment conditions. When a man was removed from the program, the circumstances were discussed in group therapy of the men, and also with the mothers. Consistent with program commitment to accountability and visibility of actions and decision making, all program participants were supported to recognize that living within the treatment agreement conditions provided an opportunity to show themselves and others they could live to these standards. In the process the men experienced conducting themselves in different ways, to a new set of standards they articulated. Their families, initially with significant direction from the program, developed ways of assessing the harming men against these standards. This was particularly so for the mothers, who are critical to the healing and well-being of their daughters.

## Community monitoring

To ensure the safety of children and community confidence in the program a procedure was developed for checking that the harming fathers were complying with the conditions of their treatment agreement. As the program was a diversion from the usual sentencing options the Probation and Parole authority was not available. Nor were the Police with the exception of the Child Protection Register, which did not provide the level of monitoring needed. A private company was contracted to undertake checks to ensure the harming parents were living in their approved residences, were not having contact with children unless approved, or otherwise not keeping to their conditions. At times family or others provided information regarding non-compliance, which precipitated targeted checking. At other times, when the men appeared 'stuck' and not making progress in treatment a check was organized. This arrangement was discussed with the men during assessment and included in the treatment agreement. Privacy was respected as checking did not include a right to enter premises (e.g. home or workplace) or to disclose to anyone that the men were in the program (e.g. neighbours).

## Building safety

These checks confirmed serious breaches on a number of occasions including: commencing a new relationship with a single parent who moved in with her child; visits with children in the family including at times the victimized child; visiting or staying at the family home; and consuming alcohol when this was prohibited. Breaches were reported to the sentencing Court and dependent upon severity of the breach the harming father was either removed from the program and sentenced, or returned to the program with a warning or with an extension of the period of time in the program.

## Contact and reunification

Contact between the harming father and other family members follows considerable therapeutic work with the exception of 'facing up' by the harming father, which is done during the assessment or soon after. While some families anticipated family reunification, this was not the goal of the program. However if this is what a family stated they wished the program included this as part of the treatment plan. In addition to having time and therapeutic support to work through all of her personal responses to the sexual abuse, the mother is encouraged to exercise her judgement about these matters. The orientation material for mothers states the following.

### Supervised contact

Your partner may at a later stage in his treatment be able to have contact visits with your children. These visits can only occur in the presence of yourself, or another adult approved by you. Your partner will need to apply for this supervised contact. It will be approved by the program if his therapist assesses he has progressed satisfactorily through treatment and if he has provided a sufficient plan for contact. These visits will only go ahead however, if (and when) you agree to it and your child is assessed as ready.

### Reunification of the family

Whether or not your partner is ever invited back into the family is a difficult and very personal decision. The program neither promotes nor prevents your family getting back together once your partner's treatment ceases. Instead, your therapist can guide and support you through this, by helping you to deal with your thoughts and feelings so that you may be clear about your own preference regarding this issue.

While this is difficult for some mothers, the emphasis on steps being taken in collaboration with her is significant to helping her engage with the children's recovery and navigate the complexities of recovery. The orientation booklet for the men speaks directly to this issue as well:

> Family reunification is not a goal of the Program. If you wish to reunite with your family, this should be identified by yourself as an issue for treatment. All steps towards reunification should take place as part of your treatment program. You will need to develop a reunification plan and apply for each step as variations of your Treatment Agreement. We will not accept or participate in a reunification plan if it is not what everybody in your family wants.

Family reunification can take many forms. While most may assume it is the whole family cohabiting again, this is one option only. Preceding family reunification, if it is being considered, is contact. Any form of ongoing relationship can be defined as a form of family reunification. Sequencing contact between the harming father and children of the family is critical to ensure that the victimized child is not isolated, held responsible for the harming father's absence or pressured about the pace at which contact is being considered. If the pace for others is too slow, a critical issue to consider is whether the harming father has been sufficiently detailed about his sexual abuse and whether in the family, particularly the mother and victimized child have been able to reconcile regarding this.

The program did not set up a set sequence or rigid set of requirements for contact or reunification. It suggested that each family member set up a list for themselves as an outline of necessary criteria, and to also do this in relation to each other family member. Therapists joined with this process with each individual and joint work, particularly mother and daughter. This is a very dynamic process of exploring what each person would like for themselves and of each other. It can be too easy to simply ask if the family (or a child) is 'ready' as this implies contact should happen and does little except build pressure on the child.

Similarly if re-contact is built predominantly around the harming father, he may be able to work through defined steps: acknowledging his sexual abuse behaviour, living by different standards, developing improved abilities to self-regulate strong negative emotional states, distancing himself from intrusive or controlling behaviour of others, engaging an audience and practising more respectful ways of communicating with the mother. However this does not necessarily answer the question of whether contact is in the best interests of a child or is on the same timetable.

Generally the mother is always present for initial contact by the harming father and any of the children. It is important to be sensitive to the cultural needs of a family and authentic family based responses are possible as the following example shows.

> Tyrone had sexually abused his daughter Fiona over a number of years. She and her mother, brother and younger sister had individual and shared counselling for more than a year when they decided it may be time for Fiona's brother, John to meet with Tyrone ahead of some contact away from the program but with family

# 136 Building safety

> supervision. Fiona's brother was 14 years old. The family was from a Pacific Island nation and requested the meeting for Tyrone and his son be conducted in a culturally appropriate way. This meant the meeting was held not with John's mother present but her father, John's grandfather and Tyrone's father-in-law. Tyrone came prepared with some things to say in response to issues John had said he wanted covered. The grandfather listened to this and then indicated to the therapist he wished to take the lead. He then spoke to Tyrone outlining how he had seen with sadness and anger how the whole family was affected by Tyrone's actions. He said that Tyrone had taken much from his grandchildren and the mother and that while Tyrone is John's father he had given up his right to show his son what a man and father should be. He said he stepped into that role and would watch carefully as Tyrone and John were reconnecting. There was no minimization about Tyrone's sexual abuse of his daughter, strong support for John, and clarity about the family expectations of Tyrone as they now were exploring if Tyrone could re-join them.

Mothers who decided they would reunite were encouraged to commence this process during participation in the program in order that all the steps taken could be thoroughly evaluated after each step.

## Maintaining safety from re-offending after mandated treatment

### Maintenance and Support System (MASS)

Towards the end of the program the men are asked to establish their 'Maintenance and Support System' (MASS). MASS differs from audience as MASS members have ongoing defined roles in supporting the harming father, including expectation to intervene or alert others if concerns arise. Pre-dating the well-recognized 'Circles of Support' (Wilson & Picheca, 2005), this procedure is for men who have social connections and will benefit from ongoing relationships with a small group of people to support him to remain safe from re-offending. A MASS involves at least five people who are aware of the harming father's abusive actions, and of his participation in the program. These persons must be fully informed by the harming father of his safety plan, which includes risk factors or indicators of concern. They need to be persons to whom the harming father makes himself accountable and to whom he can turn for support, and with whom he maintains regular contact.

The mother is not a member of the MASS though she has input into selection of MASS members, being able to nominate one or two of the MASS members. If she plans to remain in a relationship with the harming father it is essential she is confident each MASS member will contact her if any concerns arise for them. The MASS members also raise concerns directly with the harming father; and communicate with each other and the therapist. The harming father develops a plan to present to his prospective MASS members including his intentions to continue with maintenance therapy. He meets with them as a group at the program, where sometimes MASS members meet for the first time. Ideally they are from different parts of his life so that the major contexts of his life have responsible people supporting him.

## Maintenance therapy

At the conclusion of the mandated period of participation there was an open-ended monthly group meeting that all men were encouraged to join. Most attended for a period and some for more than two years. Attending maintenance therapy was a standard many indicated to their MASS and if they stopped coming, this could initiate action by their MASS. The men attending maintenance group generally reported it as important due to the acceptance and mutual understanding when speaking with other men who had been through the program. In this group there was a difference between acceptance and comfort as the men had learnt in the course of the program to be very direct, giving and receiving feedback from each other. Respectful confrontation was a routine event and anchored in mutual recognition of holding a commitment to living without being abusive in any way.

## Ongoing safety monitoring

At Cedar Cottage, the introduction of a child protection register managed by the Police presented an opportunity to work together with Police in their community supervision role. The program was able to contribute to risk assessments, which determined level of intensity of supervision as well as confirming other relevant matters including whether the men were progressing well through the program. Indicators included attending regularly or, in the case of men post-completion, continuing to attend maintenance group as planned. This had the potential to contribute to child safety, as in the following example.

Dean travelled to Scotland with his aged mother to take his father's ashes to his birthplace. Dean advised his Crime Manager at the Police of his intention to travel overseas. The Police alerted authorities in Scotland who interviewed him on his arrival. They inspected his mobile phone as part of this procedure and found several photos he had taken of schoolchildren when he had been on a train in Sydney. This was enough to raise concerns and he was not immediately granted entry and they checked back with Australian authorities who in turn contacted the program. Dean had not attended maintenance sessions for a number of months. While the photographs were not indecent, they signalled concern about Dean. Due to the purpose of his visit Dean was allowed entry to Scotland on condition he adhere to his planned schedule, report to Police daily and undertook to contact the

## 138 Building safety

> program on his return to Australia. He also had an elevated level of reporting upon his return. The photos were an indicator of renewed sexual interest in children. This indicated to his mother and other relatives that Dean needed ongoing close management and support.

## Conclusion

Building safety begins with the first actions in responding to a referral and thereafter through therapeutic processes at every stage of the program. Of critical importance to building safety is ensuring that the mother is getting support from sources other than the harming father alone. Unless this occurs she is unable to work through all the implications of his sexual abuse of their child and develop confidence and capacity to exercise informed judgement about herself, her daughter and family relationships. Therapy is pivotal to establishing boundaries to allow this to happen and in particular to removing as many obstacles as possible to her crucial role in her daughter's recovery. For the harming father the challenges are significant as he is guided towards, but unable to be forced, to commit to responsible and respectful behaviour. This framework for building safety will make his choices transparent to all family members.

## References

Esposito, C. (2015). Child sexual abuse and disclosure: What does the research tell us? Retrieved from https://www.facs.nsw.gov.au/__data/assets/file/0003/306426/Litera ture_Review_How_Children_Disclose_Sexual_Abuse-.pdf

Jenkins, A. (1990). *Invitations to Responsibility: The Therapeutic Engagement of Men who are Violent and Abusive.* Adelaide, South Australia: Dulwich Centre Publications.

White, M. (2005). Workshop notes. Retrieved from https://www.dulwichcentre.com. au/michael-white-workshop-notes.pdf

Wilson, R. J., & Picheca, J. E. (2005). Circles of support and accountability: Engaging the community in sexual offender risk management. In B. K. Schwartz (Ed.), *The Sex Offender: Issues in Assessment, Treatment and Supervision of Adult and Juvenile Populations* (Vol. 5, pp. 13–11–13–21). Kingston, NJ: Civic Research Institute.

Wyre, R. (1990). [Ethos Statement, Personal Communication].

# Chapter 10

# Group work

## Introduction

Across all types of human service intervention there is widespread recognition that group work can play a pivotal role in reducing isolation and facilitating recovery. We found this to particularly apply to work with parental child sexual abuse for harming fathers, child victims and mothers because of the high degree of stigma and secrecy which exists. This chapter describes the group work programs that were conducted at Cedar Cottage.

Irving Yalom, a foundational author on therapeutic group work identifies 11 primary interdependent factors at play in therapy groups. Of these, seven were present in the work of Cedar Cottage groups: i) instillation of hope from observing others with same problems at greater stage of 'recovery'; ii) a sense of universality from discovering that others share the same predicaments, 'all being in the same boat'; iii) imparting information; iv) opportunities to experience altruism; v) interpersonal learning, from learning about oneself through the relationships formed; vi) group cohesiveness, from finding acceptance after sharing one's inner world; and vii) catharsis, through opportunities to safely express feelings (Yalom, 2005). Groups can also be very empowering for those who have been disadvantaged, oppressed or experienced problems which are hidden, providing voice and counter-acting the dynamics of isolation and secrecy which individual therapy can create.

## Groups for harming fathers

### Evidence for groups for harming fathers

Most treatment programs for those who sexually offend are offered through groups (Schmucker & Lösel, 2015). Group therapy has been the recommended treatment for many years, because of the opportunities provided for peer support and confrontation (Newbauer & Hess, 1994). In practice, this creates difficulties in determining the relative impact of group therapy on offenders, as distinct from individual therapy. Other identified advantages to using groups in treatment of those who sexually harm include: opportunities to address common interpersonal deficits and develop new skills such as conflict resolution, communicating emotions, learning about one's impact on others; experiences of positive feedback, support, vicarious learning and alleviation of stigma (Ware, Mann, & Wakeling, 2009). Disadvantages of groups include: risks of reinforcement of criminal attitudes, opportunities to learn new techniques for offending or fantasies and establishment of problematic networks (Ware, Mann, & Wakeling, 2009). Offenders themselves report that group work on its own as a treatment modality risks a 'one-size fits all' approach and emphasize the need for tailoring intervention to individual's needs (Colton, Roberts, & Vanstone, 2009).

A meta-analysis of treatment programs for those who sexually offend suggests that multi-systemic treatment models have better outcomes and that a mix of both individual and group sessions may yield the strongest results in reducing recidivism (Schmucker & Lösel, 2015). The literature also points to some pertinent considerations in delivery of group therapy, which include: the value of team approaches, including both male and female group facilitators and the importance of supervision (Rich, 1994). The therapeutic relationship is found to be an essential element in the establishment of groups for those who sexually offend, being more consistently related to engagement in group therapy than offender characteristics (Holdsworth, Bowen, Brown, & Howat, 2014).

Offenders themselves perceive group therapy as useful, with one small study of 32 men in outpatient treatment reporting a preference for group over individual therapy, identifying benefits to include opportunities to share experiences, learn from and relate to others, receive support, and experience confrontation (Garrett, Oliver, Wilcox, & Middleton, 2003). In another study of 338 participants in community outpatient group treatment programs, most appreciated the experience of being able to share their experiences with others (Levenson, Macgowan, Morin, & Cotter, 2009). Emotional engagement in offender group therapy is also found to be achieved when participants trust their peers and feel respected by therapists (Willemsen, Seys, & Gunst, 2016).

### The Cedar Cottage harming fathers groups

Group therapy for harming fathers is an integral part of the Cedar Cottage model, with a requirement for attendance at a fortnightly group meeting in addition to weekly/fortnightly individual therapy and other conjoint sessions as indicated. The groups were replaced twice yearly with intensive workshops to focus on particular skill development issues, with one of these series being held over the summer break when many of the men face additional loneliness, being excluded from family celebrations at which the children are present.

The purpose of a group work element of treatment is to provide opportunities for:

- Developing perspective taking;
- Improving communication skills;
- Development and practise of self-regulation;
- Peer support;
- Exploration and testing of beliefs by peers; and
- Providing a safe environment for practising and reviewing self-evaluation.

Groups for men attending Cedar Cottage were structured as open groups, with participants entering and exiting groups as they joined and completed the program. Up to three groups for men were provided at any time, with one group established specifically for new participants and other groups for those who were further progressed in their treatment. In this way, the men experienced a sense of progression. Groups ran for semesters of ten weeks and the membership of the two more advanced groups was settled at the start of each semester while the new participants' group accepted new members whenever new members joined the program. Group membership was reviewed and determined at the start of each semester. Groups provided opportunities for new participants to learn from those who have participated for longer in the program, and to celebrate the achievements of those who successfully completed. Small group sizes of four to seven members ensured sufficient space for all and prevented participants 'hiding' in a larger group, which is a risk of using only the group treatment modality with those who sexually offend. There was also a practice of groups accepting single session visits from men during their assessment, which the visitor reported to be a positive and encouraging experience.

Wherever possible, groups for harming fathers should be co-facilitated by a male and female therapist. This provides the opportunity to model gender equity and respectful ways of relating between men and women. As has been observed elsewhere, attending to the dynamics of the gender of therapists helps the harming father to uncover beliefs about gender that may also be linked to past, inappropriate ways of behaving sexually (Rich, 1994). As found by Willemsen, Seys and Gunst (2016), groups were a useful forum for harming fathers to increase their emotional awareness and expression. Contrary to the widely held view that men are reluctant or unable to talk about their feelings, we found them to be highly articulate in expressing their emotions with one another in the context of group therapy.

At Cedar Cottage the format for sessions involved a group round in which each participant provided their name, an acknowledgement of and brief details of who (by relationship) they harmed, the impact of their actions, current family status and their hopes for future including what they aimed to achieve in their therapy. The round also included a catch-up activity called 'The Walk' in which participants physically stepped out on the floor in the centre an event from the past fortnight which provided an example of putting personal safety strategies into practice, that is – a warning sign or difficult situation was identified, the predominant feeling named, the consequences of acting on the impulse anticipated and action taken to address the risk. Group work sessions should not focus on sexual abuse accounts or sexual content, which is reserved for individual sessions. In our experience, it is unhelpful for the men to be aware of the details of each other's offending, as this can provide material for unhelpful thought patterns. Where participants are preoccupied with sexual themes, it is the problem and process for interrupting the thoughts that is discussed, rather than the content.

To ensure accountability and transparency, a report should be made after every group session by the facilitators which documents: group members present (noting absences); session format; changes made to session plan; focus and issues raised in session; process between group members; process between therapists and group members; therapists' overall evaluation of session; issues to be followed up at next session; plan for next session. In addition, a report for each individual group participant is required documenting their preparation and participation. This includes: punctuality, clarity of the participant in relation to his goals for treatment, evidence of reflection between sessions, clarity about the topic he proposes for discussion, degree and quality of group participation. This report forms part of the clinical record of the harming father and can be important to assessing progress. At Cedar Cottage, these reports were also presented at fortnightly meetings dedicated specifically to group review. The process of completing the report after each group session also acts as an important de-brief for facilitators prior to departing after, typically, evening group meetings.

A fortnightly group work meeting at Cedar Cottage, attended by all therapists, provided a forum for accountability for the harming fathers' group work program, including keeping the child/ren's and family's needs in focus, as well as to facilitate coordination and planning, skills and theory development through sharing, and to identify any issues for training, research or supervision.

One of the risks of providing group therapy to harming fathers is the opportunities provided for collusion and reinforcement of pro-offending beliefs and behaviours. For this reason, treatment agreements of harming fathers specify that contact with group participants outside the group sessions is not permitted. Accordingly: exchanging telephone numbers; meeting before or after the group sessions; comparing therapy notes; travelling to and from sessions together; and working together were not permitted. Each of these exclusions was specified following incidents with participants who breached this 'no contact' rule. A second risk we addressed through the group rules was breaching confidentiality for other group members: in discussing the group with others, participants were not to name other participants.

Men who completed the Cedar Cottage Program could choose to attend Maintenance Group on a voluntary basis. This monthly, open group provided a valued avenue of support and maintenance of safety strategies and was well used by a number of program completers. Participants in this group also took turns to visit the new participants group each semester, providing hope and a sense of perspective to those starting out.

## Groups for mothers

### Evidence for groups for mothers of children who have experienced sexual assault

Mothers whose children experience sexual abuse find it extremely difficult to express their doubts about their abilities as mothers with social workers when workers may be making judgements about their 'ability to protect' and support groups provide a safe and non-judgemental forum to express these fears (Hill, 2001). The high degree of concurrent abuse directed towards the mother by the harming father, with 36 per cent in one study indicating abuse (32 per cent emotional and 20 per cent physical) (Hiebert-Murphy, 2001) points to the need to create space for the women's own needs to be met, as harmed individuals in their own right, as well as mothers. As outlined in Chapter 4 there are many barriers to mothers responding with support to their child after parental sexual assault. These factors may be more readily addressed in a group where women feel better understood and less judged than in encounters with professionals.

### The Cedar Cottage mothers' groups

From the outset of contact with a program, it is useful for mothers to be aware that there will be opportunities to meet with others who have experienced the effects of parental sexual assault. At Cedar Cottage these groups allowed for development of a unique support network among women sharing the same stigmatizing isolation. Chances to meet other mothers in a space where honesty, trust, openness and understanding with respect for confidentiality, were seen as essential to supporting these women's journey. Because there were no concerns about collusion and promoting unhealthy thinking, in contrast to the harming fathers' groups, there was no restriction on mothers sharing contact details or meeting up before or after sessions, and the development of a support network was actively promoted. In our experience, the mothers' groups provided a forum of inestimable value to this group of women, profoundly cutting through the isolation they experienced as a result of their partner's abuse of their child/ren.

Significant challenges exist in providing groups for mothers from one agency, for which creative solutions are required. A first challenge is that it is not unusual for mothers and children to live a long distance from the program, either because the harming father has elected to travel, for what is highly specialized treatment, or because she has elected to re-locate with the children to create a new life. A second challenge is that not all mothers wish to participate in group therapy, even under conditions of confidentiality. The reasons for this include: the impacts of enduring shame; eroded self-esteem as a result of abuse by the harming father; reluctance to engage with the agency as a means to create distance from the harming father; or prior close engagement with a victim support agency. Some mothers are initially hesitant to attend groups, being under the sway of the harming father, but after some months have changed their perspective. Often this occurs following the harming father's revelations in therapy about the extent of his sexual abuse and accompanying tactics of manipulation and secrecy that can fuel her anger. At such a point many women have an increased desire to connect with other women in the same situation. Unlike the harming fathers, mothers always have parenting obligations, so child care and arrangements for a diverse range of ages of children add to the complexity of timetabling. Because of these factors, creating a sufficient critical mass of mothers to create an effective group is not always straightforward. A minimum of four participants is required to create the dynamics required for group engagement and for cohesion to develop. As it is typical for at least one potential participant to withdraw or not attend, in effect groups require a minimum of 5–6 participants to commence. Unlike those provided for the harming father, mothers' groups are most usefully offered as closed groups over a shorter time frame. This recognizes the complex demands on the lives of mothers, who are juggling competing needs of an abused child and their siblings, as well as work force obligations and providing for the family.

A solution to these challenges refined at Cedar Cottage over a period of many years of trial and error was to offer parallel groups for mothers and children as intensives over several days. Such 'intensive' or workshop format groups can be offered three times a year to coincide with school holidays allowing greater access for distant families and reducing the burden on the mothers. Parallel groups also allow conjoint group sessions to occur in which the mothers and children together participate in activities and discussions, which address the universal dynamics of secrecy, loyalty, responsibility and resistance. A combination of psycho-education, activities and age appropriate discussion proves a very potent tool to safely discuss issues that neither mother nor child will comfortably raise. The wider audience of other mothers and children also helps normalize the predictable fears and reactions that both mothers and children experience. The costs for mothers of attending these intensives can sometimes be defrayed with funding from child protection agencies, or the harming father, where this is acceptable to the mother.

Co-facilitation by two female therapists modelled women as holders of authority and helped to build trust in the group. An exception to this was that each group cohort was offered the opportunity for the Program Director to attend a session of the group to answer their questions. This was done after it was requested by participants in the first mothers' group. In a group setting, bolstered by other women, the opportunity to interrogate the Director about aspects of the program and its intentions for the harming father and the family as a whole, was experienced as empowering by the women. An indication of the value placed by women who participated in these groups and the unique opportunities they provided for reassurance and decreased isolation is found in the following comments by two mothers who participated in groups at Cedar Cottage and who participated in a study of mothers' and daughters' experiences of the program (Laing, 1996).

> Yeah, you're sharing with these women that become a real support group. There's not really anyone else you can talk to unless they've been in the situation. I mean your friends are helpful, but how can they know what it's like for you?
> Just that there's other mothers there going through exactly the same as you, the feelings, the questions, and everything. You're not alone.

## Groups for abused children

### Evidence for groups for children after parental sexual assault

Individual therapy is usually a powerful tool for those who have experienced sexual assault, however it has an unavoidable problematic aspect. The privacy, intimacy and inherent power disparity between therapist and service user replicate the dynamics of most experiences of sexual violence, with its secrecy, intensity and power imbalance. In addition to the therapeutic elements identified by Yalom and discussed in the introduction to this chapter, therapeutic groups as an intervention mode disrupt all these elements, bringing potent benefits.

Group therapy is the most favoured treatment option for children after sexual abuse (Horvath, Davidson, Grove-Hills, Gekoski, & Choak, 2014). The same review also concluded that interventions focusing on the family and not the individual child are more effective in addressing the long term impacts of intra-familial child sexual assault. This supports earlier research suggesting that children who participate in individual, group *and* family work to address the impacts of sexual abuse fare better than those who participate in any of these separately or dually (Briere, 1992). An issue to be borne in mind is that the full meaning of children's experiences may not be apparent to them when abuse occurs at a young age, but that as they mature and gain understanding of the significance of their experiences, negative impacts can be experienced. For this reason intervention for young children is warranted, focussing not only on the amelioration of current symptomatology but on the prevention of potential difficulties (Berliner & Wheeler, 1987 cited in Deblinger, Stauffer, & Steer, 2001).

Common process and outcome goals for group programs with sexually victimized children include:

# 146  Group work

- Clarifying and validating conflicting and ambiguous feelings associated with the abuse and aftermath of disclosure;
- Facilitating expression of thoughts and feelings contained during the experience;
- Universalizing and detoxifying the experiences through appropriate sharing;
- Exploring explanations for the abuse that help the child organize her feelings
- Teaching age-appropriate methods for eliciting, expressing and receiving nurturance and physical affection;
- Enhancing the child's sense of control, bodily integrity and efficacy;
- Establishing protective strategies for future risk situations. (Sturkie, 1992)

In line with the prevalence of parental sexual abuse and the experience at Cedar Cottage, the children who had experienced parental sexual abuse were girls. Most of the literature on groups for children after sexual assault accordingly addresses girls. In relation to unique needs for boys, it has been suggested that their gender-specific defence mechanisms typically involve unsafe, aggressive behaviours which require concrete interventions to connect this to the sexual abuse (Scott, 1992). Accordingly separate groups for boys provide space to address issues of male power, identification with the person who abused them, and the particular issues of stigma and shame they experience (Case, 1992). We concur with this view and propose that children's groups should be gender specific. This also provides the opportunity to deal with specific issues of stigma and shame experienced by girls and boys.

Diverse models of group work have been applied to groups for children after sexual assault. In a comparison of supportive groups versus groups employing cognitive behaviour therapy (CBT), it was found that the mothers and children who experienced CBT demonstrated better outcomes than those who participated in supportive group therapy (Deblinger et al., 2001). The study found that children who attended both types of group had reduced post-traumatic stress disorder symptoms, intrusive thoughts and child behavioural problems and the authors note that the CBT groups employed more interactive approaches and included a mother–child component of each group, which we suggest may have contributed significantly to stronger outcomes (Deblinger et al., 2001). Narrative approaches have also been employed in group work for children, seen by proponents as a valuable approach for children to develop ideas about the nature of abuse, its impact on their lives, and ways of resisting its effects (Want & Williams, 2000). Such approaches often employ parallel groups recognizing the inclusion of mothers as a way to shift from seeing facilitators as experts, increasing transparency, and providing an audience to the steps children are taking (Want & Williams, 2000). Despite considerable evidence of therapeutic groups being offered extensively for children after sexual assault, evidence of their effectiveness remains scant, though a large review concluded that the children themselves favour group approaches in intervention (Horvath et al., 2014).

### The Cedar Cottage children's groups

From the outset children's groups offered important opportunities for the children harmed by men attending Cedar Cottage, and early on we sought to offer these in parallel to mothers' groups wherever possible, in light of the challenges identified for the mothers' groups.

Group work programs for children at Cedar Cottage employed narrative therapy approaches and the four key dynamics we see as underpinning child sexual assault which were outlined in Chapter 2 – secrecy, responsibility, protection/loyalty and resistance – were addressed. Accordingly, sessions in the children's groups were dedicated to each of these, in turn exploring how secrecy was imposed, ways in which the children were led to feel responsible for the abuse, how their desire to protect others had been manipulated and finally but importantly, ways in which they resisted the prescriptions imposed by the abuser.

The core shared experiences and unmet needs of the children's group are dealing with the impact of sexual abuse by a parent and re-building the mother–child relationship. Apart from these two key elements, other different perspectives and needs will emerge in group, for which a shared experience cannot be assumed. For example, in Laing's study (1996), one girl raised the issue of combining girls who were biological and step-daughters of the offenders in the same treatment groups, since she saw this resulting in the girls having quite different goals:

> Sometimes it was difficult. Some of the girls said things all the time about 'I hate my father' sort of thing, and that was difficult, 'cause everyone else was trying to get it all back together and stuff.

Although there were differences in perspective such as this, the experience of meeting with other girls who have been sexually abused by their fathers was always welcoming and safe. To hear diverse perspectives and needs from other girls was seen as critically important for each girl in her own recovery. Exploring some ideas and expressing herself in a group, sometimes strongly, was often safer than in individual sessions. Also, it was helpful to hear at times, another girl putting together the words that accurately reflected an aspect of themselves which, up until that time, they had not been able to articulate as fully.

Compared to mothers' groups, planning for children's groups requires a number of additional considerations. In particular, the children's age and developmental stage is a key consideration for inclusion criteria, given disparate needs and perspectives across age groups. At Cedar Cottage, the youngest abused

# 148  Group work

child seen was six years and the oldest 17, a span which precluded inclusion in the same group. At the same time, we found the girls at Cedar Cottage far more generous than might normally be expected in terms of a workable age span, with early high school aged participants tolerating late primary school aged girls in the same group, and adapting to their developmental needs with a flexibility we would not expect in other contexts. Working with small numbers, we also found positive outcomes in running a group as small as three participants, though this approaches a small group counselling model rather than traditional group work.

Another strategy we employed to achieve a critical mass was to co-facilitate groups with other child sexual assault service providers and include children who had experienced sexual abuse by non-family members. With care and attention to the individual needs of the diverse participants, this can be a successful model. We found, however, that girls deeply valued being with other girls who had experienced abuse by their own father.

## Conclusion

Group work is not an adequate stand-alone intervention for any family member affected by parental sexual assault. However, as part of an integrated approach to treatment along with individual, conjoint therapy and where relevant, family sessions, it forms a potent forum for harming fathers to establish and maintain accountability for their actions. Concomitantly, for mothers and victimized children, groups provide unique empowering opportunities to speak freely with others who have had similar experiences and to be understood in a setting without stigma or shame. The possibilities these experiences provide for forging safety are not to be under-estimated.

## References

Briere, J. N. (1992). *Child Abuse Trauma: Theory and Treatment of the Lasting Effects.* Thousand Oaks, CA: Sage Publications.

Case, J. (1992). Meeting others: Group work for children who have been sexually abused. In J. Breckenridge & M. Carmody (Eds.), *Crimes of Violence: Australian Responses to Rape and Child Sexual Assault.* Sydney: Allen and Unwin.

Colton, M., Roberts, S., & Vanstone, M. (2009). Child sexual abusers' views on treatment: A study of convicted and imprisoned adult male offenders. *Journal of Child Sexual Abuse, 18*(3), 320–338. doi:10.1080/10538710902918170

Deblinger, E., Stauffer, L., & Steer, R. (2001). Comparative efficacies of supportive and cognitive behavioral group therapies for young children who have been sexually abused and their nonoffending mothers. *Child Maltreatment: Journal of the American Professional Society on the Abuse of Children, 6*(4), 332–343.

Garrett, T., Oliver, C., Wilcox, D. T., & Middleton, D. (2003). Who cares? The views of sexual offenders about the group treatment they receive. *Sexual Abuse: A Journal of Research & Treatment, 15,* 323–338.

Hiebert-Murphy, D. (2001). Partner abuse among women whose children have been sexually abused: An exploratory study. *Journal of Child Sexual Abuse, 10*(1), 109–118. doi:10.1300/J070v10n01_06

Hill, A. (2001). 'No-one else could understand': women's experiences of a support group run by and for mothers of sexually abused children. *British Journal of Social Work*, 31(3), 385–397.

Holdsworth, E., Bowen, E., Brown, S., & Howat, D. (2014). Offender engagement in group programs and associations with offender characteristics and treatment factors: A review. *Aggression and Violent Behavior*, 19(2), 102–121

Horvath, M., Davidson, J., Grove-Hills, J., Gekoski, A., & Choak, C. (2014). *It's a Lonely Journey: A Rapid Evidence Assessment on Intrafamilial Child Sexual Abuse.* Retrieved from London, UK: http://eprints.mdx.ac.uk/13688/1/Its%20a%20lonely%20journey_final%20%282014%29.pdf

Laing, L. (1996). *Unravelling Responsibility: Incest Offenders, Mothers, and Victims in Treatment.* (PhD), The University of New South Wales, Sydney.

Levenson, J., Macgowan, M., Morin, J., & Cotter, L. (2009). Perceptions of sex offenders about treatment: Satisfaction and engagement in group therapy. *Sexual Abuse: A Journal of Research and Treatment*, 21(1), 35–56.

Newbauer, J. F., & Hess, S. W. (1994). Treating sex offenders and survivors conjointly: Gender issues with adolescent boys. *The Journal for Specialists in Group Work, 19*(2), 129–135. doi:10.1080/01933929408413772

Rich, K. (1994). Outpatient group therapy with adult male sex offenders: Clinical issues and concerns. *Journal for Specialists in Group Work*, 19(2), 120–128.

Schmucker, M., & Lösel, F. (2015). The effects of sexual offender treatment on recidivism: An international meta-analysis of sound quality evaluations. *Journal of Experimental Criminology*, 11(4), 597–630. doi:1.library.unsw.edu.au/10.1007/s11292-015-9241-z

Scott, W. (1992). Group therapy with sexually abused boys: Notes toward managing behavior. *Clinical Social Work Journal*, 20(4), 395–409.

Sturkie, K. (1992). Group treatment of child sexual abuse victims: A review. In W. T. O'Donohue & J. H. Geer (Eds.), *The Sexual Abuse of Children: Clinical Issues* (Vol. 2, pp. 331–364). Hillsdale, NJ: Lawrence Erlbaum Associates.

Want, C., & Williams, P. (2000). Adventures in groupwork. *Dulwich Centre Journal*, 1 & 2, 10–16.

Ware, J., Mann, R. E., & Wakeling, H. (2009). Group versus individual treatment: What is the best modality for treating sexual offenders? *Sexual Abuse in Australia and New Zealand*, 1, 70–79.

Willemsen, J., Seys, V., & Gunst, E. (2016). "Simply speaking your mind, from the depths of your soul": Therapeutic factors in experiential group psychotherapy for sex offenders. *Journal of Forensic Psychology Practice*, 16(3), 151–168.

Yalom, I. (2005). *The Theory and Practice of Group Psychotherapy.* New York: Basic Books.

Chapter 11

# Creating safety for doing the work

## Introduction

Therapeutic work with children who experience sexual abuse or with adults who perpetrate it is demanding – intellectually, emotionally and spiritually. This work poses significant professional, organizational and personal challenges which ultimately call on the humanity of practitioners. Work with those who sexually harm children is not suited to all therapists, whether social workers, psychologists or psychiatrists and it is relevant in a book of this nature to address the question of who should and should not undertake this work. It is also important to address how intervention needs to be structured to support therapists in undertaking this work.

## Responding to the reactions of others

Working with people affected by sexual assault and, in particular, with those who have sexually assaulted children carries reputational and identity implications for the therapist. Child sexual abuse evokes strong personal responses. The goal of integrated work in parent–child sexual abuse is commonly misunderstood as reunification. Therapists can be faced with views of family, friends and colleagues doubting the value of doing this work and misplaced assumptions about the therapist's values. This extends at times to questions about the therapist's ability to avoid being tricked or manipulated by harming fathers and assumptions that by working with harming fathers they are 'on the other side' and acting against the interests of victimized children. Therapists should anticipate people expressing their opinions about doing this work.

When challenged about choosing to do this work, we have found that a useful response is often to pose a question: 'Do you think something should be done about this problem (of parent–child sexual abuse)?' After then explaining that the situation is legally and interpersonally complex and that permanent removal or imprisonment of the harming father is not possible, many people concur that something does need to be done. It can be very effective to simply say: 'I am one of the people trying to do something (about this problem).'

Navigating the personal and professional implications of this work is a matter for every therapist. Unfortunately, much of the literature focussing on work-force issues presumes that undertaking this work results in (1) ongoing vicarious trauma experiences, which are inevitable and which (2) the therapist must manage. Neither of these is automatically the case.

An alternative perspective is taken by practitioners such as Vikki Reynolds who concludes that it is witnessing the persistent social injustices encountered by clients, far more than encounters with clients themselves, that cause workers to 'burn out' (Reynolds, 2011). As Reynolds observes, connecting with the wider social justice implications of this work, along with others involved is an essential aspect of participating in this field and contributes not only to social change but to sustaining and creating durability amongst practitioners.

## A framework for safety

To focus as a starting point on the qualities of individual therapists carries the risk of over-estimating the responsibility of the individual therapist to manage the complexities of this work. Instead we propose a framework for safety which recognizes three elements:

1   The nature of intervention for parent–child sexual abuse;
2   The context for parent–child sexual abuse;
3   The therapist.

### The nature of intervention for parent–child sexual abuse

Acknowledging the nature of parent–child sexual abuse includes recognition of the dynamics of child sexual abuse, central issues of the harming father's responsibility for these assaults and ways in which he may attempt to transfer this to others, and harm done to the child, their siblings, the mother and all familial relationships. Parent–child sexual abuse is a form of gendered sexual violence. The nature of this work means addressing: inequality and disadvantage through the misuse of power and authority, deception, exploitation and coercion as well as the explicit sexual beha-viours and their impact on dependent children and people close to them, especially their mothers.

### The context for parent–child sexual abuse intervention

Responding to parent–child sexual abuse occurs within different legal and interagency contexts. How therapeutic work is offered, under whose authority and to whom the work is accountable, is strongly related to workforce issues. How is the work valued? What are the standards and treatment goals of an agency or socio-legal system? An agency responding to parental child sexual assault

## 152 Creating safety for doing the work

has a responsibility to take into account the nature of parental sexual abuse in program design, therapist caseloads and professional support including provision of training and supervision. Individual therapist qualities cannot mediate badly designed or poorly supported therapeutic service delivery systems. A therapist is unlikely to be able to sustain themselves undertaking this work in isolation and without support. The societal, statutory, service and legal responses to child sexual assault can have as much or greater impact on workers than direct work with children and families.

The agency has responsibility for putting in place the therapeutic program structure including protocols for service delivery, orientation and training of staff. Credentialing therapeutic staff is a significant issue as specialist training and prior experience in this area of practice is not broadly available. The approach an agency brings to these matters substantially influences the context within which this work is undertaken and the ability of therapists to work effectively.

Therapists within an organization should not be left totally responsible to manage their responses to undertaking the work. Therapists working in private practice are at greatest risk as they carry a higher level of responsibility to put their own support structures in place. An issue to be kept in mind in considering the content of this work is the impact on non-clinical staff in agencies dedicated to this work. Not uncommonly staff members such as those in administration support roles experience pervasive thoughts about child sexual abuse, as a result of exposure to written material, team discussions and informal debriefing by clinical staff. A well designed agency will have orientation and business procedures including supervision support in place tailored to the specific needs of each staff designation. Only after these two elements of work practice are considered, and planned for, do the qualities of the therapist come into consideration, as outlined below.

### The therapist

As noted by Judith Herman (1981), therapy with people who sexually assault others differs markedly from traditional forms of therapy, which presume a client who is suffering distress, who seeks help voluntarily, and holds nothing back. In contrast, harming fathers do not experience distress, as long as they have sexual access to a child, rarely seek help voluntarily, and conceal much in their behaviour.

Harming fathers are likely to seek to restore or retain their position within the family, continuing to use the same interpersonal strategies they used in sexually harming the child when engaging in therapy. To be able to work effectively with harming fathers requires a paradigm shift, which is not within the range of all therapeutic practitioners. While a general principle of therapeutic work is for the therapist to adopt a position of neutrality, this does not mean being neutral about child sexual abuse. It is a matter of ethical practice that therapists are clear about the harm and responsibility for child sexual abuse.

Therapists working with parents who harm need to acknowledge the disclosures, expressed feelings and stated intentions of this client group while recognizing these may include inaccuracies, minimizations and other limitations. Therapists also need to hold empathy for the harming father, as well as for every other family member. If a therapist is unable to recognize a harming father as a person capable of change, therapeutic efforts are unlikely to be effective as the therapist places him or herself in a position of constantly being suspicious of the harming father's motives and authenticity. Doing this work well requires a significant ethical and emotional 'stretch' on the part of therapists. Unless empathy can be harnessed for harming fathers, therapists will be unable to demonstrate the warmth and genuineness that is required to engage any client in therapeutic work.

A further critical quality required of therapists engaging in work with those who harm children is the ability to hold multiple perspectives. A hallmark of those who sexually abuse children is their inability to hold multiple perspectives, clinging instead to their own viewpoint, with an inability to experience and express empathy (Simons, Wurtele, & Heil, 2002). Developing capacity for remorse and victim empathy are aims of offender treatment, but are also considered to be difficult skills to instil and maintain (Colton, Roberts, & Vanstone, 2009). Those who work therapeutically with harming fathers need to be able to canvas, identify and hold multiple perspectives on the same events. The therapist needs not to be taken in by the harming father's interpretation of events while maintaining an expectation that he is able to progressively take responsibility for his actions, consistent with his standard of doing so and not leaving the victimized child with any level of responsibility. It is also necessary to be clear that holding multiple perspectives does not mean the therapeutic outcome is a negotiated or mediated agreement to maintain those differences. The essence of victim-centred practice in parent–child sexual abuse is to anchor therapeutic processes to the reality of the child's sexual abuse and not accept that this is negotiable.

Gender of therapists is always an issue, given the gendered nature of sexual violence. For male therapists, issues include responding to attempts by harming fathers to co-opt them into discourses about masculinities, including definitions of women and children in relation to men, around concepts like: 'how women are' or 'how these things happen'. In teams that provide therapy to mothers and child victims, gendered power imbalances, which intervention seeks to address, can be replicated when the therapist – automatically in a position of power – is also male. The gender of the service provider is often relevant for those who have experienced sexual abuse (Hooper & Warwick, 2006). While this does not preclude men as therapists, these issues need to be at the forefront in this work. Women therapists may have to deal with misogyny, or at least attitudes which diminish or objectify girls and women by harming fathers. Women therapists may also become subject to sexualized attention or objectification by clients.

## 154    Creating safety for doing the work

> Danielle's client Max, in his journal in which he was asked to track his day to day activities, wrote about sexual thoughts he was having about Danielle including reference to what he found to be physically attractive about her. A client having sexual thoughts about their therapist is not uncommon. It is relevant to Max's therapy. How he communicated this to Danielle is relevant as well. Whether Danielle is comfortable in dealing with this in therapy sessions with Max and how the agency supports Danielle are the relevant issues.

Equally likely are assumptions on the part of harming fathers that women in the agency hold less power and responsibility than their male counterparts. For both male and female therapists, as Rich (1994) observed, challenges are posed for them as a workforce to collaborate, as well as to model equitable gendered relations in front of a highly observant and critical client group.

### Therapist's personal experiences of abuse

The personal impact of therapy with abusers is of particular relevance for those who have themselves experienced violence. The prevalence of personal experiences of abuse is high in the population as a whole and there is evidence that rates may be higher among helping professionals. In a survey of 303 Californian child protection workers, approximately one-half reported experiencing physical and/or sexual violence by an intimate partner, one third reported physical abuse, and 22 per cent sexual abuse during childhood (Mieko & Mills, 2003). Amongst 1,981 nursing staff, 18 per cent reported that as a child they had experienced 'being touched in a way they did not wish to be touched, or forced into sexual activity (any kind)' (Bracken, Messing, Campbell, La Flair, & Kub, 2010, p. 140). In the same study, approximately 25 per cent reported lifetime prevalence of intimate partner violence.

All therapists working in this field need to examine their values, experiences and conscious and possibly unconscious biases they bring to the work. Previous experiences of abuse render workers particularly vulnerable to experiencing distress though they may also provide greater clarity and understanding. In either case, therapists with personal experiences of abuse should ideally declare this in commencing this work, in order to receive appropriate supervision and support. Agencies employing therapists also hold responsibility to ask about relevant values, experiences and beliefs during the recruitment process, rather than rely on the individual to raise these matters in the process.

## Staying safe

Therapists undertaking direct trauma-based practice commonly report secondary trauma as a result of their work. Indirect exposure to violence through hearing accounts of child sexual abuse or other traumatic material is recognized as a potential cause of post-traumatic stress. For example, a survey of 282 social workers involved in direct practice with traumatized populations, found that 55 per cent met at least one of the criteria for post-traumatic stress disorder and 15 per cent met all three core diagnostic criteria (Bride, 2007). Another study, which focussed specifically on practitioners providing therapy for sex offenders, found that a sample of 86 mental health practitioners working in this field reported higher levels of emotional exhaustion and depersonalization, but also personal accomplishment, compared to the general population of mental health workers (Stoddart, Taylor, Shelby, Stoddart, & Taylor, 2001).

One of the risks for therapists in this field is being manipulated by the harming father, which Herman (1981) suggests is the goal of most harming fathers in treatment. Persuading the therapist to side with him as an underdog and take on the role of advocate, ally or protector, can and has assisted many harming fathers from avoiding prosecution, taking responsibility for their behaviour, or getting access rights to their children.

> Referral processes at times were rapid, occurring a few weeks after disclosure but more usually 2–4 months had passed. A program applicant, who was a therapist himself, had commenced therapy after being charged and before referral to the program. He brought a report to the assessment from the therapist which said: 'I have been impressed with Mr Jones' sincere approach to his therapy. I do not have prior experience working with incest offenders. Mr Jones has been helpful by providing me with books on the subject from his library.'
>
> In this way Mr Jones' therapist had been influenced to accept Mr Jones as a subject matter expert. This maintained Mr Jones in his regular dynamic of being in control of the process but distanced him from being able to identify and address his beliefs and conduct.

Staying safe in treating offenders involves three key strategies: teamwork, a code of limited confidentiality, and interagency response. Each of these is discussed in turn.

Firstly, this is work which is best undertaken in teams in order to provide the transparency, reflexivity and support we believe is required. As a minimum if work is being offered to the range of family members, this cannot be undertaken by a single therapist. It is necessary for mothers and victimized children to have an independent advocate who does not also have primary responsibility for the harming father's therapy. Regular clinical supervision, as well as team collaboration enables frequent, regular review of case progress and issues of the therapist and harming father therapeutic relationship. We propose both individual as well as group supervision no less than monthly, in addition to formalized and regular client review processes to be conducted weekly as part of a team. Every client of course does not need to be discussed weekly but a process of team review and working through a schedule of client reviews supports healthy team processes. This is an agency responsibility and the review processes need to be well planned, conducted in a respectful and safe manner and be reliable. Safety is essential for therapists when reviewing their clinical work with each other and the process needs to be predictable and valued. Cancelling meetings such as this shows they are low priority and devalues them. Engaging in regular review processes ensures consistent progress towards treatment goals and identification of boundary violations or other unhelpful processes which may impede progress. In addition, agencies must ensure that an employee assistance program or equivalent is in place to provide independent, anonymous counselling support for workers.

Secondly, all work with harming fathers, their victims and other family members, must be carried out within the bounds of a shared understanding that limited confidentiality applies to all work. This is consistent with good therapeutic practice, in particular, practice which may include children at risk. When all participants in therapy understand the need for, and actively practice limited confidentiality, the risk of collusion and development of 'special relationships' with harming fathers, victims or other family members is reduced. Alongside this code of practice is the requirement that therapists have capacity to work within a mandated treatment context. Although in effect, much therapeutic work is experienced by service users as 'mandated', for example couple counselling, parenting skills development and substance use treatment, the criminal nature of sexual offending renders this a very specific domain, as regards confidentiality, attendance and progress.

Finally, interagency responses provide needed transparency and accountability to treatment of harming fathers. Without an external accountability mechanism, it is too easy for individuals and teams treating offenders to develop an ever-narrowing field of vision, which risks isolation and adoption of discourses of 'specialness', not being well understood by other agencies or systems and self-justifying practices. The need for some form of statutory oversight was outlined in Chapter 2.

Another measure which brings needed openness and scrutiny to even the best-intentioned of this work is establishment of an oversighting advisory or reference group. Such a group can comprise representation of statutory child protection and/or law enforcement agencies, victims' rights groups or services and, if relevant, funding bodies.

## Conclusion: holding onto one's humanity

Therapy with those who have sexually harmed children offers to the therapist extraordinary power over their client. This is the case whether the work is mandated by a court with the power to sentence and imprison the harming father, or private practice, where the stigmatized identity may still be widely revealed. This situation offers to the therapist a sense of power that is unusual and at times hard to resist. The discourse of heinousness which accompanies sexual offending can fuel self-righteousness among therapists, leading them to justify to themselves intervention that is confrontational, coercive or punitive.

What becomes apparent to a reflective therapist is that unless one's own sense of humanity is maintained in undertaking this work, we are reduced to being at the same level as the abusers, that is, no better than those we purport to 'help'. An additional important framing is the power attributed to the privileged position of the therapist. The therapist needs to be able to recognize the privilege and responsibility of their position. They have power in relation to harming fathers which should not reflect the dynamic of how the harming father misused the power he held in relation to his child victim. These imperatives are reflected in the work of those who have influenced our work, including Alan Jenkins who argues that intervention with men who harm others must move beyond attempts to coerce, confront or educate unwilling and unmotivated clients. Instead Jenkins (2009) argues for three elements of respectful intervention which comprise:

- Assisting men in finding an ethical basis and the means to cease abusive behaviour and to develop new ways of relating;
- Being informed by political, rather than psychological, metaphors of explanation and understanding;
- Seeing intervention in terms of power relations and practices within families and communities.

Our approach is influenced by Jenkin's work and employs an invitational approach to work with harming fathers to set standards for themselves and employs a power analysis which disinclines towards use of 'power over' tactics on the part of therapists. Marshall and colleagues (2005) also caution against overly confrontational therapeutic styles, for the simple reason that they are not effective. Instead they propose that change is facilitated by empathy, warmth, encouragement, rewards for progress and a degree of directedness, and argue that a lack of rapport between offenders and clinicians, or fragmented and mechanistic treatment delivery are counter to effective intervention (Marshall et al., 2005). Drawing on this work, Hackett (2006) reinforces the importance of therapists' use of self to create a positive relationship, rather than reliance on manualized approaches which can become stale and defensive. Hackett also notes that given the centrality of power to sexual abuse, it is important for therapists to examine their own sources of power which involves attending to: the existence of power imbalances in one's own relationships – both personal and professional; willingness to consider how one's power is used and experienced; critical openness about one's own values and behaviour, in particular in relation to gender, sex and sexuality (Hackett, 2006).

## References

Bracken, M., Messing, J., Campbell, J., La Flair, L., & Kub, J. (2010). Intimate partner violence and abuse among female nurses and nursing personnel: prevalence and risk factors. *Issues in Mental Health Nursing*, 31(2), 137–148.

Bride, B. (2007). Prevalence of secondary traumatic stress among social workers. *Social Work*, 52(1), 63–70.

Colton, M., Roberts, S., & Vanstone, M. (2009). Child sexual abusers' views on treatment: A study of convicted and imprisoned adult male offenders. *Journal of Child Sexual Abuse, 18*(3), 320–338. doi:10.1080/10538710902918170

Hackett, S. (2006). The personal and professional context to work with children and young people who have sexually abused. In M. Erooga & H. Masson (Eds.), *Children and Young People Who Sexually Abuse Others: Current Developments And Practice Responses* (2nd ed., pp. 237–248). Abingdon, Oxon: Routledge.

Herman, J. L. (1981). *Father–Daughter Incest*. Cambridge, Mass: Harvard University Press.

Hooper, C. A., & Warwick, I. (2006). Gender and the politics of service provision for adults with a history of childhood sexual abuse. *Critical Social Policy*, 26(2), 467–479.

Jenkins, A. (2009). *Becoming Ethical: A Parallel, Political Journey with Men Who Have Abused*. Dorset, UK: Russell House.

Marshall, W., Ward, T., Mann, R., Moulden, H., Fernandez, Y., Serran, G., & Marshall, L. (2005). Working positively with sexual offenders maximizing the effectiveness of treatment. *Journal of Interpersonal Violence*, 20(9), 1096–1114.

Mieko, Y., & Mills, L. G. (2003). When is the personal professional in public child welfare practice?: The influence of intimate partner and child abuse histories on workers in domestic violence cases. *Child Abuse & Neglect*, 27(3), 319–336.

Reynolds, V. (2011). Resisting burnout with justice-doing. *International Journal of Narrative Therapy & Community Work*, 4.

Rich, K. (1994). Outpatient group therapy with adult male sex offenders: Clinical issues and concerns. *Journal for Specialists in Group Work*, 19(2), 120–128.

Simons, D., Wurtele, S. K., & Heil, P. (2002). Childhood victimization and lack of empathy as predictors of sexual offending against women and children. *Journal of Interpersonal Violence, 17*(12), 1291–1307. doi:10.1177/088626002237857

Stoddart, R., Taylor, K., Shelby, R. A., Stoddart, R. M., & Taylor, K. L. (2001). Factors contributing to levels of burnout among sex offender treatment providers. *Journal of Interpersonal Violence*, 16(11), 1205–1217.

# Index

'accidental' touching of children 75
Accountability 2, tactics aim to avoid, minimize accountability 21, 24, 62 ; offender accountability operationalized to avoid mother-blaming 57; questions to victim that place accountability on the harming father 80, of harming father for the abuse and undermining family relationships 81, 86, central to safety 122–123, 142
additional sexual assaults: ethics of treatment and community supervision 51–53; process for identifying additional victimized children 28; responding to disclosures by siblings 91–92
admitting offender: tactics *see* tactics of harming father;
alienation 38
amelioration phase 37
Apology that mutualizes responsibility 59; offering an immediate apology 62; child pressured at accept premature apology 85; different to accountability 100–101;
assaults, additional: disclosure of 51–53
assessment, building safety into 122–133; accountability 122–123; assessment interviews 50; community monitoring 133–134; developing a complete account of the abuse 124–128; establishing an audience to change 128–129; goals, standards and plans of action 123–124; treatment agreement 130–133
audience, concept of 116; establishing an audience to change 128–129
autonomy of child, respecting/restoring 83–84

Bancroft, L. 8
Barrett, M. J. 59
Blake, R. H. 35, 37
Bolen, R. M. 26, 62, 64
boundary violations 38–39, 107
boys, abuse of 4, 5, 9, 27, 54, 91, 146
bribery 36
Briere, J. N. 6
brothers *see* siblings

Caffaro, J. 95
Carlton, R. 62
case management, safety factors 48–49
Cedar Cottage Program, Sydney 1, 2–4, 26–30, 61; children's groups 147–148; criminal rehabilitation 13; duration of operation 3; establishment 2; group work 139–145, 147–148; harming fathers' groups 140–143; as integrated treatment model 99; legislation 45; mothers' groups 143–145; narrative approaches to therapy 12, 25; nature and severity of sexual offending 27; preparedness to return men to court 29–30; and re-offending 28–29; requirements regarding harming father 3, 9, 84; research 17, 26, 28; responsibility, adoption of 9; and reunification of family 3, 29; sources 9; and tactics of harming father 76; Treatment Agreements 3; withdrawal from 29–30
child protection 3, 26, 61; agencies 21, 23, 102, 144; authorities/services 46, 62, 63, 78, 79, 102; interventions 62–63; investigations 47, 62, 79; literature/texts 57, 58; orders 109; registers 133, 137; reports 52, 92; statutory 156; workers 35, 127, 154

# 160 Index

children: autonomy of, respecting and restoring 83–84; non-offending parent, rebuilding fractured relationships with 81–83; resistance by 25; role in harming father's treatment 51; sexual abuse of *see* parental child sexual abuse; sexual abuse of children; *see also* victimized children

Christianson, J. R. 35, 37

'Circles of Support' 136

cognitive behaviour therapy (CBT) 146; *see also* Trauma-Focussed Cognitive Behavioural Therapy (TF–CBT)

cognitive distortions 13, 20

collaboration 22

communication: attempts to communicate with victim 41; covert 40, 44, 45; between siblings 94–95

community monitoring 133–134

community supervision and treatment, ethics of: access by siblings to the harming father 51; admissibility of assessment material in court 49–51; children's role in treatment of harming father 51; disclosure of additional assaults and victims 51–53; and ethics of treatment 49–53

complex trauma 11

confidentiality 22

conjoint work 1, 67, 83; harming father–daughter work 109–111; harming father–mother (parent dyad) work 101–106; harming father–siblings work 107–109; mother–daughter–siblings work 107; mother–daughter work 106–107; role within integrated treatment 100–101; victim-centred family approach 22

Coohey, C. 6

co-responsibility, belief of 37

court: admissibility of assessment material in 49–51; preparedness to return men to 29–30

covert communication 40, 44, 45

*Crime Description* 124–125

culpability, maternal 57–60, 63

data 5, 8, 29; outcome 28; prevalence 26, 53; *see also* research

daughters: harming father–daughter work 109–111; mother–daughter–siblings work 107; mother–daughter work

106–107; predominance in parental incest 9

denial 34, 73, 78, 102, 123, 128; and engaging the harming father 41, 42, 45, 47, 48; and siblings, issues relating to 90, 96

deprivation 38

Dessel, A. B. 64

disclosure of incest: additional assaults and victims 51–53, 91–92; barriers to, set up by harming father 77; by child experiencing parental sexual assault 76–79; crisis 32–34, 60, 61–63, 90; mandatory reporting 52; moment of 32; motivations 77; as process 78; by siblings, responding to 91–92; tactics of harming father post-disclosure 40–42; and therapeutic engagement 47; working with families following 23

disconnection 11

discovery of parental sexual assault 76–79, 90

domestic violence 10, 25, 59, 120

dynamics in child sexual abuse, key 23–26; at societal level 25–26

dysfunctional families 57, 59

Easton, S. 6

effects of sexual abuse 4, 6, 11, 25, 48, 69, 143; and engaging the harming father 48, 53; experiences of children suffering parental sexual assault 72–76, 80, 81; by women 53

Elliott, D. M. 6

empathy 60, 63, 86, 153, 157

engaging the harming father 32–56; disclosure, crisis of 32–34; ethics of treatment and community supervision 49–53; initial goals and standards 46; legislative support for engagement 45–46; in meaningful therapy 45–48; tactics 35–45; therapeutic engagement 46–48; useful questions 47; "why" question 34–35

entitlement 11

environment, sexualizing 39–40

ethics: practice of approaching former victims 118–119; of treatment and community supervision *see* community supervision and treatment, ethics of;

*Ethos Statement* 18, 122, 123, 124

## Index 161

evidence, group work: for children following parental sexual assault 145–147; for harming fathers 139–140; for mothers 143

extended family: anger, guilt and prior abuse issues 119–120; approaching former victims, ethics and practice 118–119; bringing others in on story 115–117; grandparents, work with 114–115; harming father's siblings as earlier victims 117–118; loss of 113–114; loss of connection to 96; non-harming fathers 119; safety, intervention for 120; work with 113–117

external controls, importance 21

extortion 36

extra-familial offenders 7

'facing up' by harming father 85–87, 110, 111; meetings 100–101, 105, 106

false statements, alleged 41

family dysfunction 58, 59

family meetings 3, 107

*Father–Daughter Incest* (Herman) 11

fathers: biological/non-biological 27, 113; father–child relationship 27; harming *see* harming father; non-harming 119

favouritism 38

female perpetrators 5, 53–54

feminist empowerment 25

feminist research 10–11, 60

films, with sexual content 39

Finkelhor, D. 5

force/violence, use of 37; *see also* domestic violence; physical abuse

former victims: anger, guilt and prior abuse issues 119–120; approaching 118–119; harming father's siblings as 117–118

Fraenkel, P. 64

gender factors in child sexual abuse 4–5, 10

Giaretto, A. 10

Giaretto, H. 10, 59

gifts 33, 36, 38, 91

Goodwin, S. 60

grandparents, work with 114–115

grooming 35, 36, 44

group work 22, 139–149; abused children, groups for 145–148; Cedar

Cottage Program 147–148; evidence for 139–140, 143, 145–147; for harming fathers 139–143; for mothers 143–145, 147

Gunst, E. 141

habituation 40

Hackett, S. 157

harm: by fathers *see* harming father; inter-generational 115; by mothers 53–54

harming father: access by siblings to 51; attitudes towards women and children, determining 20; barriers to disclosure set up by 77; boundaries, contained by 20; children's role in treatment of 51; committing to a formal agreement 20; compared to harming mother 54; conjoint work 107–109; engaging 32–56; ensuring continued commitment by 20; external mandate important to support the work 20; facing and demonstrating responsibility 20; 'facing up' by, preparing child for 85–87; groups for *see* harming father, groups for; inadvertent attribution of power to 44–45; life-long risk of re-offending 21–22; motivations/reasons for behaviour 34–35; personal history, exploring all aspects 20; preparedness to return to court 29–30; preparing child for 'facing up' by 85–87; safe re-contact with 84–85; siblings of as earlier victims 117–118; step-fathers 113; tactics *see* tactics of harming father; taking responsibility for all aspects of his abuse 19; terminology 9; unsupervised contact with 97

harming father, groups for 139–143; Cedar Cottage Program 140–143; evidence for 139–140

harm minimization 12–13, 42–43

Herman, J. 9, 10–11, 152, 155

Hill, A. 96

humanity, holding onto 156–157

Huppatz, K. 60

incest, parental *see* parental child sexual abuse

incidents of abuse 27

individuation 39

informed consent 52

## 162 Index

integrated treatment 99–101; conjoint work, role within 100–101; victim-centred family approach 17–18
inter-generational harm 115
interventions for parent–child sexual abuse 3, 59, 96, 120; child protection 62–63; context for 151–152; nature of 151; victim-centred family approach 18, 19; *see also* therapeutic work with mothers; therapeutic work with siblings; therapy/therapeutic approach
intra-familial child sexual abuse *see* parental child sexual abuse
intra-familial violence, and parental sexual abuse 8
investigations 47, 62, 79

Jenkins, A. 12, 34, 35, 101, 157

Kellogg, N. D. 8
Kelly, L. 10
Krane, J. 62

Laing, L. 147
Lev-Weisel, R. 59
limited confidentiality 22
'Lolita myth' 11
Loyalty as key dynamic of child sexual abuse 25

Maintenance and Support System (MASS) 136–137
maintenance therapy 21–22, 137
male victims 4, 5, 9, 27, 54, 91, 146
mandated treatment 22, 136–138
marital stress 35
Marshall, W. 12, 157
masculinity, alternative notions of 12
Maynard, S. W. 8
monitoring: community 133–134; ongoing 137–138
mother–child relationship, undermining 59, 69; and engaging the harming father 38, 40; tactics of harming father 38, 73, 74, 81; victim-centred family approach 25, 27; *see also* mothers
mothers 57–71; absence of 58; blaming for abuse by fathers 24–25; collusive 59; courtship with, attempts to re-ignite 33, 43; groups for 143–145, 147; harm by 5, 53–54; maternal culpability 57–60, 63; maternal sexual

unavailability 43–44; mother–daughter–siblings work 107; mother–daughter work 106–107; non-offending, as never to blame 1, 19; re-evaluation of relationship with partner 68; resuming of sexual relationship with partner 68; therapeutic work with 63–69; 'unwitting accomplice' 59; *see also* mother–child relationship, undermining

Nagy, V. 7
narrative approaches to therapy 12, 25, 79, 146
natural justice, principles of 50
Nelson-Gardell, D. 77–78
New South Wales (NSW), government response to prevalence of child sexual assault 2
non-offending parent: allocation of responsibility to 57; importance of engaging 11; mothers, as never to blame 19; non-harming fathers 119; rebuilding fractured relationships with 81–83; terminology 9
nudity 39

O'Leary, P. 6
online material, sexually explicit 39
oral abuse 27
*Orientation Booklet* 123, 134–135
'outsider-witness' 129

paedophilia 9
parental child sexual abuse: children experiencing 72–88; context 24; co-occurrence with other forms of intra-familial violence 8, 89; disclosure *see* disclosure of incest; discovery *see* discovery of parental sexual assault; features 7; groups for children who have experienced 145–147; intervention 151–152; invisibility of parental incest 4–5; less dangerous than other sexual offences against children, myth of 1, 8–9, 13; levels of risk 8; multiple perspectives of perpetrators 153; multiple types of act 27; other forms of child sexual abuse compared 6–8; prevalence 4–5; and sibling relationships 95; *see also* interventions;

## Index 163

sexual abuse of children; victimized children
parent dyads 101–106
partner violence 10
patriarchy 10
penetrative abuse 27
Pereda, N. 4
Phelan, P. 75
physical abuse 8, 23, 154; *see also* force/violence, use of
physical environment, manipulating 39
post-disclosure tactics 40–42
post-modernism 12
Post-traumatic Stress Disorder (PTSD) 84, 146, 155
power: abuses of 8, 21, 157; imbalances/inequalities 5, 10, 12, 25, 50, 157; inadvertent attribution of, to harming father 44–45; misuse of 151; of therapist 153
*Pre-Trial Diversion of Offenders (Child Sexual Assault) Act, 1985* (NSW) 2, 51
Pre-Trial Diversion of Offenders Program *see* Cedar Cottage Program, Sydney
procedural fairness 50
Proeve, M. 91
projection 25
protection: as key dynamic of child sexual abuse (see loyalty) 25; child protection *see* child protection; dynamics of 26; of siblings 25
psychometric tools 8

Quadara, A. 7
qualitative research 60

reactions of others, responding to 150–151
readiness 12
recidivism *see* re-offending
Reid, B. 36
relapse prevention planning 13
re-offending: Cedar Cottage Program 28–29; life-long risk of 21–22; rates of 17
research 4, 7, 10, 77, 124; Cedar Cottage Program, Sydney 17, 26, 28; data 5, 8, 26, 28, 29, 53; extended family work 113–114; feminist 60; group work 142, 145; mothers 62, 64; qualitative 60; recidivism 28, 29; victim-centred family approach 17, 23, 30

resistance, as key dynamic of child sexual abuse 25, 77, 79–81
response-based approaches to therapy 12, 25, 81
responsibility: acceptance of 12; for all aspects of abuse, taking 19; allocation of 57, 60; Cedar Cottage Program approach 9; children experiencing parental sexual assault 79–81; co-responsibility, belief of 37; demonstrating 20, 21; key dynamic in child sexual abuse 24–25; misplaced, for child sexual abuse 26; shifting onto others 24, 35
reunification of family: Cedar Cottage Program 3, 29; and contact, safety factors 134–136; forms 135
Reynolds, V. 151
Rich, K. 154
risk assessment 48–49
Risk–Need–Responsivity (RNR) model 13
Ritchie, D. 8
*Royal Commission into Institutional Responses to Child Sexual Abuse,* Australia 26
Russell, D. 4–5, 53, 54, 114

safety factors: assessment, building safety into 122–133; building of safety 122–138; case management 48–49; contact and reunification 134–136; creating safety while doing the work 150–158; immediate child safety, focus on 62–63; interventions 120; maintaining safety from re-offending following mandated treatment 136–138; maintenance therapy 21–22, 137; ongoing monitoring 137–138; reactions of others, responding to 150–151; re-contact with harming father 96–97; safety framework 151; safety of victimized child, other family members and potential future victims 18; staying safe 154–156; supervised contact 134
Salter, A. 93
Sarles, R. 58
second wave feminist theory 10, 26
secrecy 19, 79–81, 107; key dynamic in child sexual abuse 24–25; enforced 24
self-interest, of harming father 41, 64

## 164 Index

sexual abuse of children: age of onset 5; assessment, building safety into 122–133; boys 4, 5, 9, 27, 54, 91, 146; context for intervention 151–152; developing a complete account of 124–128; disclosure/discovery 76–79; and domestic violence 25; dynamics 23–26; effects see effects of sexual abuse; experiences of harming father's tactics 72–76; gendered nature 4–5, 10; grooming see grooming; impact of harming father's tactics 72–76; incidents 27, 34; intentionality 21; meta-analyses 5, 6; nature and severity of sexual offending 27; parental and others forms compared 6–8; penetrative abuse 27; prevalence 2, 4–5; reporting of 52, 79; terminology 4, 9; US statistics 5; see also parental child sexual abuse
sexual arousal of the child 37–38
sexual violence 10
Seys, V. 141
Sgroi, S. M. 58
Shame 37, 47, 54; of mothers 63, 64; of mothers resuming a sexual relationship with their partner 68; for child as barrier to disclosure 75; shame for siblings at disclosure 90
Sheinberg, M. 64
siblings 51, 89–98; communication between 94–95; disclosure/discovery 90; experiences of, in relation to harming father's tactics 91; of harming father, as earlier victims 117–118; needs and roles, in therapeutic work 92–96; protection by victimized child 25; rebuilding fractured relationships with 81–83; relationship with victimized child 83; responding to disclosures of further sexual assaults 91–92; safe re-contact with harming father 96–97; younger, understanding of abuse by 108
silencing tactics 24, 25
Silverman, J. G. 8
sisters see siblings
Staller, K. M. 77–78
standards 46
step-fathers, abuse by 113
Stoltenborgh, M. 4
Strega, S. 62

supervised contact 134
Sutter, J. 64

tactics of admitting offender: courtship with the mother, attempts to re-ignite 33, 43; explicit and implicit explanations 43–44; harm minimization 42–43; mutuality 42; therapeutic questions to identify the limitations of admission 44
tactics of harming father 7, 35–45, 90; attempts to communicate with victim 41; boundary violations 38–39; covert communication 40; denial 41; efforts to influence others close to the victim 41–42; experiences/impact 72–76; and experiences of siblings 91; extortion 36; favouritism vs alienation and deprivation 38; force/violence, use of 37; misunderstanding 44–45; mother–child relationship, undermining 38, 73, 74, 81; post-disclosure 40–42; sexual arousal of the child 37–38; sexualizing the environment 39–40; silencing 24, 25; victim-centred family approach 24
teamwork 22–23
television, with sexual content 39
therapeutic work with mothers 63–69; engagement and initial phase 63–65; unravelling tactics and re-evaluating important relationships 65–69
therapeutic work with siblings: additional issues 95–96; beliefs 93–94; existing communications with harmed child, establishing 94–95; extended family, loss of connection to 96; knowledge 93; needs and roles 92–96
therapists 152–154; gender 153; humanity, holding onto 156–157; personal experience of abuse 154; teamwork 22
therapy/therapeutic approach: broad scope for therapy 20; cognitive behaviour therapy (CBT) 146; confidentiality 22; different approach to therapeutic relationship 22; external controls, importance 21; group therapy see group work; life-long risk of re-offending, recognition of 21–22; maintenance therapy 21–22, 137, 143; narrative approaches to therapy 12, 25,

79, 146; response-based approaches to therapy 12, 25, 81; responsibility, demonstrating 21; specialist approaches 23; teamwork 22–23; translating principles into foundations of therapeutic approach 20–23; *see also* therapeutic work with mothers; therapeutic work with siblings; therapists
thinking errors 13, 20
touching or fondling, sexual 27, 75
transparency 142
trauma 6, 9, 52, 53, 151; complex 11; Post-traumatic Stress Disorder (PTSD) 84, 146, 155; re-traumatizing the child 92, 100, 110; secondary 154
Trauma-Focussed Cognitive Behavioural Therapy (TF–CBT) 84
Treatment Agreements, Cedar Cottage Program 3
Trepper, T. S. 59
trust issues 22

victim-centred family approach 17–31; dynamics in child sexual abuse 23–26; each family member able to see perspectives of others 19; integrated treatment 17–18; intervention most effective when perspectives of all family members understood 19; needs of victimized child to prevail in decision-making 18–19; non-offending mother, as never to blame 1, 19; possibility of working with whole family 19; principles underpinning 18–20; recognizing what others have been

subjected to 19; reviewing what victim has been subjected to 19; safety of victimized child, other family members and potential future victims 18; therapeutic, foundations 20–23; *see also* victimized children
victimized children: attempts to communicate with 41; Cedar Cottage children's groups 147–148; efforts to influence others close to 41–42; and external controls 21; groups for 145–148; and needs/role of siblings in therapeutic work 92–93; needs to prevail in any decision-making 18–19; numbers victimized by one offender 27; possibility of working with whole family without sacrificing needs of 19; predominance of daughters 9; privacy rights 115; process for identifying additional victimized children 28; relationship with siblings 83; respect for choices of 85; and reunification of family 29; safety of 18; in therapy at another agency 84; *see also* parental child sexual abuse; sexual abuse of children; siblings; victim-centred family approach
violence, use of *see* force/violence, use of; physical abuse

Willemsen, J. 141
women, violence against 10, 25; *see also* mothers
World Health Organization (WTO) 4

Yalom, Irving 139

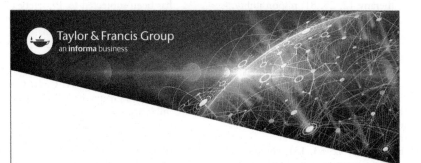